D0386841

The Lion First Bible

FOR TYLER
and the new generation

The Lion
First Bible

Pat Alexander
Pictures by Leon Baxter

LION
Children's Books

Published by
Lion Publishing plc
Mayfield House, 256 Banbury Road,
Oxford OX2 7DH, England
www.lion-publishing.co.uk
ISBN 0 7459 3210 X (hardback)
ISBN 0 7459 3849 3 (paperback)
ISBN 0 7459 3689 X (white gift edition)
ISBN 0 7459 3776 4 (red gift edition)
ISBN 0 7459 3777 2 (blue gift edition)

First hardback edition 1997
20 19 18 17 16 15 14
First paperback edition 1997
10 9 8 7 6 5 4 3 2 1

A catalogue record for this book is available
from the British Library

Printed and bound in Singapore

Contents

Old Testament Stories

1   How the World Began   10
The story of Creation
GENESIS 1 AND 2

2   The First Sad Day   20
The story of Adam and Eve
GENESIS 2 AND 3

3   Rain, Rain, Rain   28
The story of Noah and the Flood
GENESIS 6-9

4   The Promise   38
The story of Abraham
GENESIS 12-22

5   Rebecca's Wedding   48
The story of Isaac and Rebecca
GENESIS 24

6   The Troublesome Twins   56
The story of Jacob and Esau
GENESIS 25-27

7   Jacob Runs Away   66
The story of Jacob
GENESIS 28-33

8   The Jealous Brothers   74
The story of Joseph
GENESIS 37

9   Joseph Meets the King   82
The story of Joseph and his family
GENESIS 39-50

10   A Princess and a Baby   92
The birth of Moses
EXODUS 1 AND 2

11   The King Who Said No   100
The story of Moses in Egypt
EXODUS 2-12

12   The Big Adventure   110
The escape from Egypt
EXODUS 13-19

13   The Best Way to Live   120
God's covenant with his people:
the Ten Commandments
EXODUS 19-40

14   The Land of the Giants   130
The story of the twelve spies
NUMBERS 13 AND 14

15   Joshua Wins the Day   138
The battle of Jericho
JOSHUA 1-6

16   Farmer Gideon's Men   148
The story of Gideon and the Midianites
JUDGES 6-8

17   The Lion-Killer   156
The story of Samson
JUDGES 13-16

18   Ruth's New Family   164
Ruth's story
FROM THE BOOK OF RUTH

19   One Dark Night   172
The story of young Samuel
1 SAMUEL 1-3

20   The King Who Was Shy   180
The story of Saul
1 SAMUEL 8-10

21   David and the Giant   188
The story of David and Goliath
1 SAMUEL 17

22 Best Friends 200
The story of David and Jonathan
1 SAMUEL 18-20

23 The Outlaw 206
The story of David
1 SAMUEL 21—2 SAMUEL 1

24 King David's Great Idea 214
The plan for the temple
1 CHRONICLES 17 AND 22-29

25 Solomon the Magnificent 222
The story of King Solomon
1 KINGS 1-11

26 A Very Hungry Time 232
The story of the prophet Elijah
1 KINGS 17

27 Elijah's Big Day 240
The story of Elijah and the prophets
of Baal
1 KINGS 18

28 The Girl Who Helped 248
The story of Naaman's cure
2 KINGS 5

29 A Very Scary Time 256
The story of King Hezekiah and
the Assyrians
2 KINGS 18 AND 19; ISAIAH 36

30 A Fishy Story 264
FROM THE BOOK OF JONAH

31 When the Lions Roared 272
FROM THE BOOK OF DANIEL

32 A New King 281
ISAIAH 9 AND 11

New Testament Stories

33 Mary and the Angel 284
The coming of the Son of God
MATTHEW 1; LUKE 1

34 The Very Special Baby 292
The birth of Jesus
LUKE 2

35 Presents for Christmas 302
The visit of the Wise Men
MATTHEW 2

36 Where Is Jesus? 310
Jesus in the temple
LUKE 2

37 Down by the River 316
John the Baptist; Jesus' baptism
MATTHEW 3

38 Twelve Special Friends 322
Jesus chooses the Twelve
MATTHEW 4, 9 AND 10

39 The Very Scary Storm 330
Jesus calms the storm
MARK 4

40 The Two Houses 334
The Sermon on the Mount
MATTHEW 5-7; LUKE 6 AND 12

41 A Great Idea 342
Jesus heals a paralysed man
MARK 2

42 The Kind Soldier 346
Jesus heals the officer's servant
MATTHEW 8; LUKE 7

43 Jesus and the Little Girl 350
Jesus brings Jairus' daughter back to life
MARK 5

44 A Farmer Went to Sow... 356
Parables of God's Kingdom
MATTHEW 13

45 The Big Picnic 364
The feeding of the 5,000
JOHN 6

46 "Help! Help!" 370
The story of the good Samaritan
LUKE 10

47 The Lost Sheep 378
...and the Good Shepherd
LUKE 15; JOHN 10

48 Lost–and Found 386
The story of the prodigal son
LUKE 15

49 "Our Father..." 392
Jesus teaches about prayer
MATTHEW 6; LUKE 18

50 The Best Party Ever 398
The story of the great feast
LUKE 14

51 "Who Am I?" 404
The Messiah; Jesus transfigured
MATTHEW 16 AND 17

52 "I Can See!" 410
Blind Bartimaeus
MARK 10; JOHN 8

53 A Nasty Little Cheat 414
Zacchaeus the tax-man
LUKE 19

54 Little House at Bethany 418
Martha, Mary and Lazarus
LUKE 10; JOHN 11

55 A Donkey for the King 422
Palm Sunday and after
MATTHEW 21 AND 26

56 A Last Meal Together 428
The Last Supper
MATTHEW 26; JOHN 13 AND 14

57 The Saddest Day 436
Good Friday–the crucifixion
MATTHEW 27; MARK 15; LUKE 22-23; JOHN 19

58 The Happiest Day 442
Easter Day–Jesus' resurrection
MATTHEW 28; MARK 16; JOHN 20-21

59 Jesus Goes Home 452
The ascension
ACTS 1

60 When the Wind Blew! 456
Pentecost–and the Holy Spirit
ACTS 2

61 Peter's Story 460
ACTS 1-12

62 Paul Meets Jesus 466
ACTS 8-9

63 Shipwreck! 470
ACTS AND THE LETTERS

64 A New World 476
REVELATION 21

Where to find...

The quotations in this book 479

First mention of key people
in this book 480

A Word to Parents and Teachers

Creating this book has been a real challenge: staying close to the Bible text and at the same time choosing words and concepts that very young readers can understand.

But the Bible is rich in story, and story can be understood at many different levels. So I never doubted that it could be done.

Even the youngest child can enjoy and learn from these wonderful stories about the creator-God who loves and cares for his people. Love, trust, promises broken or kept, help in trouble, doing wrong and being forgiven, are key concepts in the one "big story" the Bible tells. And all are within the grasp of young children: not in the abstract, but embedded as they are in stories about people very like ourselves although they lived so long ago.

Enjoyment and understanding go hand-in-hand. So I hope you will share my own pleasure as you read these stories to and with children. The reading is meant to be interactive, helped by rhythm, repetition and the sounds evoked. It's intended to be fun! I have provided footnotes here and there by way of explanation, and to help you answer questions.

I have not "translated" every challenging word. Some – God's "Kingdom", for example – remain as bridges, making connections, ready for the time when children go on to read the Bible for themselves. No Bible story book can ever be a substitute for the "real thing": this one is meant to be a first step on the way. I hope it lays a good foundation.

My thanks to all who have encouraged and given me generous help, especially David (sometimes chewing over problems at breakfast!); friend and author, Mary Batchelor; teachers Christine Cousins and Tricia Cowell; my editor, Su Box; and artist Leon Baxter, who has done for this book what words alone could never do.

Pat Alexander

Old Testament
Stories

1

How the World Began

Close your eyes tight. Now it's all dark.
Cover your ears. Now it's all quiet.

Long long ago, before the world began,
everything was dark, everything was
quiet.
No people.
No birds.
No animals.

Then God spoke:
  "Let there be light! Let there be day.
Let there be a sun to shine."

And the light came.
How good the light was.

God kept the dark for night-time;
he made the moon and stars to shine
in the dark.

That was good too.

God said:
   "Let there be sky and land and sea."
And so it was.

But the world was still empty and quiet.

God said, "Now we must have plants."
And the first green things began to grow.
Soon there were flowers and trees and
good things to eat.

But there were no creatures to enjoy them.

So God spoke again. And at God's word,
the sea was alive with fish and swimming
things. The sky was bright with the flash
of wings. And from the earth came every
kind of animal.

Now it wasn't quiet any more!

"Chirrup! Chirrup! Cheepie-cheep!"
The birds sang for joy.

The animals tried out their voices.
Every one was different.

"Eee-aaw!" That was the donkey.

"Woof! Woof! Grrr-oof!" That was
the dog.

But still God had not finished making things.

God's beautiful new world needed people: people to look after it, people to enjoy it. People who could think and feel, like God, and make things too.

So God made the first man and the first woman, to look after the world and one another, and to love God.

The man was called Adam and the woman was called Eve.

In the beginning, when the world was
new, *everything* was good. And God was
very pleased.

After all that work, God took a rest,
to enjoy what he had made.

"God made the sky above
and the earth below.
God's love is for ever.
God made the sun for the day,
the moon and stars for the night.
God's love is for ever."*

"The earth and everything in it,
the world and all its creatures,
belong to God
because God made them."

* References for the paraphrased Bible passages
can be found at the back of the book.

2

The First Sad Day

In the very beginning, when God made the world and everything was good, there were no sad days.

God made the beautiful garden of Eden
for Adam and Eve to enjoy and take care of.
Adam and Eve loved one another, and
God was never far away. So they were
very happy.

God said they could eat any of the juicy fruit from the trees in the garden—all except one. That would not be good for them. If they ate it, bad things would happen.

But there is always someone who wants to spoil things.

One sunny day, the sneaky snake came and hissed in Eve's ear:

"Take no notisss of what God sayss. He's jussst being mean. The fruit of the tree iss good to eat. It will make you as clever asss God."

Eve looked at the tree with its rosy, juicy fruit. She wanted to be as clever as God. So she reached up to pick it.

And she ate.

Eve gave some to Adam. And he ate the fruit too.

But that very evening, when God came to talk to them, they both hid.

"Why are you hiding from me?" God said. "Have you eaten the fruit of the tree I told you not to touch?"

"Don't blame *me*," Adam said, ashamed. "It's all Eve's fault."

"Don't blame *me*," Eve said, making excuses too. "It's all the snake's fault."

God looked stern and very sad.

"Then the snake will be punished,"
God said. "But you have not done as I
told you. You wanted your own way, and
now everything is spoiled. I meant you
always to be happy. But now things will
hurt you and make you sad.

"I wanted you to live here with me always, but now you must go away – and you can't come back. You will have to work hard. You will grow old. And one day you will die."

And so it was.

Adam and Eve were very sad. But God was sadder still, because he loved them so.

3

Rain, Rain, Rain

Bang! Bang! Bang! went the hammer.

Noah was building a boat–an enormous boat.
 Big enough for all his family.
 Big enough to save two of every kind of animal and bird when the great flood came.

God was very sad about his world. It was all spoiled now. The people were so nasty and unkind. All except Noah.

Noah was nice. Noah was good. Noah was friends with God.

"I have to get rid of all this nastiness," God said to Noah one day. "The beautiful world I made is all spoiled.

"There's going to be a great flood. Enough water to take away everything that is bad. But you will be safe."

Then God told Noah to build a boat —*The Ark*.

Noah did as God said. He always did as God said.

Bang! Bang! Bang! went the hammer. At last *The Ark* was finished.

The animals were *so* excited.
   "Quack! Quack!" said the ducks.
   "Moo! Moo!" said the cows.
   "Hurry! Hurry!" said the geese.
   "Cheep! Cheep!" chirped the sparrows.
"Don't leave us behind."

   "All aboard!" said Noah. And God
shut the door of *The Ark* behind them.

A whole week went by. Then the rain
began.

Pitter, patter. Splish, splash. On and on.
Till the ark was afloat. Till the streams
filled up and the rivers ran over. More
and more rain. Till the tops of the
mountains were covered. Till there was
nothing at all to see—except water.

The Ark was alone in the world.

At long, long last, the rain stopped.
  Slowly, slowly, the water went down.
  Now Noah could see the tops of the
mountains.

The Ark came gently to rest.

Noah opened a window and out flew the raven. There was water everywhere and nowhere to land. So the raven kept on flying.

Noah waited a bit. Then he sent out the dove. She flew back with a new green leaf in her beak, and everyone cheered.

Slowly, slowly, the water went down.

Noah sent the dove out once more. This time she did *not* come back. The water had gone and the land was nearly dry.

"You can come out now," God called
to Noah. "It's quite safe. And don't worry.
There will never be another flood like
this, I promise.

"Look, I've painted a rainbow in the
sky as a sign I will never forget."

Then Noah and his family, and all the birds and animals, came out of *The Ark*.

They sniffed the good smell of the damp earth. They felt the firm ground under their feet. And they skipped and hopped and jumped for joy.

"Thank you, oh thank you, God," they said, "for keeping us all safe."

4

The Promise

The stars twinkled in the velvet black night. A billion, trillion stars.

Abraham stood outside his tent and began to count:

"One, two, three…" Had he counted that one before? He began again.

"One, two, three, four…" But he soon gave up. God was right: there were too many stars to count.

God had a special plan for Abraham.

"You must leave your home," God said, "and go to a new land. If you trust me and do as I tell you, I will give you a family *so* big they will be like the stars— too many to count. I *promise*."

A family means children, and Abraham had no children. But he trusted God and did as God told him.

So Abraham sold his house in the city of Ur. Abraham and his wife Sarah and their nephew Lot packed up for the journey. They took tents with them to sleep in.

Every day they had to find fresh grassy places for their sheep and their goats, their cows and their donkeys and their camels.

It was a long, hard journey. But, at last, they came to the new land.

"If you trust me and do as I tell you, I will give this whole land to your family," God said.

Abraham still had no children. But he trusted God and did as God told him.

There were lots more sheep now – *and* goats and cows and donkeys and camels. It was hard to find grass for them all.

"That green valley looks good," said nephew Lot, one day.

"You go there, then," said kind Uncle Abraham. "I'll move up to the hills." There wasn't much grass there for all his animals.

God loved Abraham all the more for being kind to Lot.

"Remember, *you* have my promise," God said.

"But still no children," Abraham answered sadly. They had hoped and hoped, but Abraham was growing old, and Sarah's hair was grey. Surely it was too late now to have children?

Next time God had something to tell
them he sent three men to their tent.
    Sarah baked fresh bread and cooked
the visitors a special meal.

"Before a year has gone by, you and Sarah will have a baby boy," the men told Abraham.

Sarah heard – and she laughed to herself. "I'm far too old," she said, "and so is Abraham."

"No," said the men. "You *will* have a baby. God says so."

And, before a year had gone by, the baby came.

God *always* keeps his promises.

Sarah cuddled the baby, and he chuckled and laughed. Sarah laughed too. She just couldn't help it. She was *so* happy.

Abraham tickled the baby's toes, and he laughed too. He just couldn't help it. *He* was so happy.

They called their baby Isaac.

5
Rebecca's Wedding

"We need some water," Rebecca's mother called.

"I'll go now," Rebecca said, picking up the big brown jug and setting it on her shoulder. She had to go to the well for water.

Rebecca sang as she walked. When she got to the well, she filled the big brown jug to the brim. It was very heavy now. She was careful not to spill it.

There were thirsty camels at the well.

"They must have come a long way," Rebecca thought.

She counted the camels:

"One, two, three, four, five, six, seven, eight, nine, *ten!*"

Just then, one of the men with the camels spoke to her.

"Will you give me some water to drink? "

Rebecca was careful about strangers. But this man had no jug. He looked tired and thirsty.

"Of course I will," she said. "Are those your camels? I'll get them water, too."

The man was very pleased. To Rebecca's great surprise, he opened his bag and gave her two gold bracelets.

"Please tell me who your father is," the man said. "I need somewhere to stay the night."

"My father's name is Bethuel,"
Rebecca said. And she hurried to tell her
mother.

"Bethuel!" The man could hardly
believe his ears. "My master Abraham
has a nephew called Bethuel! Thank you,
God, for helping me find him."

Rebecca's brother took care of the camels.
Her mother gave the visitor a good meal.
Then he told them why he had come.

"My master Abraham sent me here.
His son Isaac is grown up now," the man
said. "I have to find him a wife.

"I was at the well, asking God to help
me, when Rebecca came. She was *so* kind.
I'm sure she's the girl for Isaac!"

With that, he opened his bag again.
It was full of exciting presents for Rebecca
and her family.

"I must go straight back," the man said. "Can Rebecca come with me?"

"Yes," she said. "I'll come."

It was a long, long journey. But at last they arrived.

Isaac came out to meet them. Rebecca felt very shy at first. But Isaac loved her at once. There never was a happier wedding.

6

The Troublesome Twins

Jacob and Esau were twins. They had the same birthday. But Esau was born first. He was the first child in Isaac and Rebecca's family. One day, all the good things God had promised to Abraham and Isaac would be his.

But God said: "I have a special plan for *Jacob*."

Some twins look exactly alike. But Esau
and Jacob didn't even like the same
things! Esau loved being out of doors.
Jacob liked to stay at home.

Esau became a hunter. He brought home fresh meat. The smell of cooking was *so* good. His father, Isaac, loved those meals. And he was always nicer to Esau than he was to Jacob. That wasn't fair.

Their mother, Rebecca, loved Jacob best. That wasn't fair, either.

One day, while Esau was out hunting, Jacob made some delicious soup.

Esau came in starving.

"Let me have some of that," he said.

"You can have some of my soup," Jacob said slowly, "–if you let *me* be the first child, instead of you."

If Esau did that, one day all the good things God had promised would be Jacob's.

"Oh, all right," said Esau. "Have what you want. I don't care. As long as you give me some soup—I'm starving."

"Promise?" said Jacob.

"I promise." So Esau got his soup. But he soon forgot his promise.

Isaac grew old. His eyes could not see
any more. One day he called Esau to him.
    "Go out hunting tomorrow," he said,
"and cook me one of your *delicious* stews.
    "I am getting old. You are the first
child in our family. Soon you will take my
place. It's time I asked God to give you all
the good things he has promised."*

* This is the "blessing", passing on the inheritance to his son.

Rebecca overheard.
What about God's special plan
for Jacob? She didn't trust God to work
things out. Instead, she played a nasty
trick on poor old Isaac who could not see.

"I will cook him a stew—the kind he
likes best," she said to Jacob. "You must
pretend to be Esau—quick, before he gets
home."

"But Dad will know it's me," Jacob said. "Esau's hands are all hairy, not smooth like mine." Jacob was scared he'd be found out.

"Don't worry. I'll take care of that," Rebecca said.

So Jacob went to his father. He wore Esau's clothes and his hands were covered with hairy goatskin. The stew Rebecca had cooked smelled *so* good.

"Dad, it's me. Esau," Jacob said, his heart beating fast. Would he be found out?

"Surely that's Jacob's voice," Isaac said. "Come closer." He could not see, but he could feel Jacob's hands.

"Your hands are rough—you must be Esau," Isaac said. The stew smelled *so* good, he couldn't wait to taste it. "Let me enjoy this stew. Then I will ask God to give you all the good things he has promised."

So Isaac gave Jacob all that was promised to the first child. Jacob had taken Esau's place. He had what he wanted.

7

Jacob Runs Away

Jacob was running away. He wanted to stay at home, but he couldn't. His brother Esau was *so* angry at the trick Jacob had played on him.

Jacob must go to his uncle, miles and miles away.

It was getting dark now. Jacob was scared. He was all alone, and he didn't know where he was.

YEEOOUUW!

Jacob jumped. What was that? A fierce wild animal that would eat him up? Jacob was *very* scared.

When at last he went to sleep, Jacob had a dream. It was a *good* dream.

In his dream there were stairs right up to heaven, with angels going up and down them!

Then God was right there, talking to him.

"I have a special present for you," God said. "I am giving you this land. It's for you and your children and your children's children. I have a wonderful plan for the whole world. And your family is part of it.

"Don't be scared any more. You aren't all alone. I shall be with you always, and I will bring you safe home. That's a promise."

When Jacob woke up, he wasn't scared any more: he knew he wasn't all alone.

"I will love and trust you always," Jacob said to God, "if you keep your promise." He didn't know yet that God *always* keeps his promises.

Before long, Jacob was safe at Uncle Laban's house. He helped him look after the sheep.

Jacob was away from home a long, long time. He worked hard for his uncle.

And he married *both* his cousins!

Uncle Laban tricked him into marrying Leah, before he let Jacob marry Rachel, the one he really loved.

Two wives at once was not a good idea. They quarrelled over Jacob, making everyone unhappy.

Jacob had a big family–eleven boys and a girl. He had many sheep of his own. But he was sick of Uncle Laban's nasty tricks. It was time to go home.

They were nearly home when Jacob began to worry. What would his brother Esau do? Was he still angry?

"I'll send him some presents," Jacob decided. But he was still worried.

That night, Jacob could not sleep. He was all alone. But he knew God was there to help him.

"All this time God has kept me safe," Jacob said to himself. "Now he is bringing me home. Everything will be all right!"

Next day, Esau was *so glad* to see him. He hugged and kissed Jacob, and they both cried. Jacob was home again.

8

The Jealous Brothers

Joseph had a brand-new coat. His father had given it to him. It had zigs and zags and stripes—red and blue and yellow. It was a special coat, not one for every day, but Joseph wore it all the time.

"Look at me," Joseph said to his brothers. "Look at me in my new coat!"

"Dad's always giving you things. He loves you more than us. It's not fair!" his brothers shouted. Joseph had ten big brothers and one little brother. But none of *them*, not even little Ben, had a new coat like his.

Their father, Jacob, *did* love Joseph best. And it *wasn't* fair. The brothers were jealous.

Four of Joseph's brothers went out to mind the sheep. When they got into mischief, Joseph told their father.

"Nasty little sneak! Why must you always tell Dad?" his brothers yelled.

Then Joseph began to tell them his dreams.

"We were cutting the corn and tying it in bundles," Joseph said. "Your bundles bowed down to mine.

"I had another dream: the sun and the moon and eleven stars all bowed down to me."

"Who do you think you are?" his brothers shrieked. They really hated Joseph now.

One day, when his brothers were away minding the sheep, Jacob said to Joseph:

"Go and make sure everything's all right."

So Joseph set off to find them. He was wearing his special coat. They saw him coming from way away. How well they knew that coat, with its zigs and zags and stripes—red and blue and yellow.

"Here comes Dream-boy," they said. "Now's our chance to get rid of him. We can tell Dad a fierce wild animal killed him."

They were so spiteful, they wanted to kill Joseph. But Reuben tried to save him.

"Throw him down this well, instead. No need to hurt him," Reuben said.

So they tore off Joseph's coat and threw him down the well.

"Let me out! *Please* let me out," Joseph begged. But they pretended not to hear.

Then some men came riding by. Their camels were loaded with precious things to sell in far-away Egypt.

"Let them have Joseph," Judah said. "They can sell him, too."

So Joseph was taken to far-away Egypt.

The brothers made Joseph's special coat all dirty and messy. Then they went home.

"A fierce wild animal must have killed him," Jacob said, when he saw the coat. He cried and cried. He thought he would never see Joseph again.

But God had a special plan for Joseph.

9

Joseph Meets the King

Joseph was in far-away Egypt.

His wicked brothers had sent him there. His father thought a fierce wild animal had killed him.

Joseph was *in prison* in far-away Egypt. He was all alone and very unhappy.

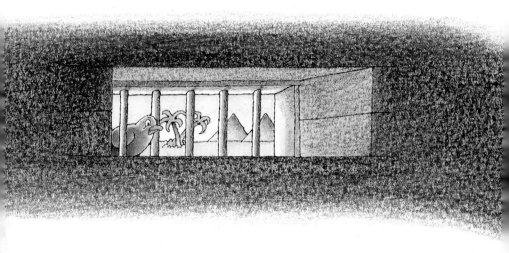

But God knew all about it. God loved Joseph and had a special plan for him.

Joseph shouldn't have been in prison.
He hadn't done anything wrong.
It was all a mistake.

The prison governor liked Joseph.
He put him in charge of all the other
prisoners.

That was part of God's plan.

One day, the king of Egypt was so cross with the man who brought him his wine that he sent him to prison.

The man was very unhappy. He had a dream that upset him.

"Tell me all about it," Joseph said. "God will help us understand."

"I had the king's cup in my hand," the man said. "I squeezed some grapes into the cup, and gave it to the king."

"That's a *good* dream," Joseph said. "It means you'll be back at the palace very soon. When you get out of prison, please tell the king about me."

"I promise I will," the man said.

Three days later, he was out of prison.
But he forgot his promise to Joseph.

Then the *king* had a dream that upset
him.
"*I* know someone who can help," said
the man who brought him his wine.
So the king of Egypt sent for Joseph.

"In my dream I saw seven fat cows by the river. Then seven thin cows came and ate them up," the king told Joseph.

God helped Joseph to understand the king's dream.

"For seven good years there will be plenty of food," Joseph said. "Then for seven bad years nothing will grow. You must store up food, so that no one is hungry when the bad years come."

"I will put you in charge, just to make sure," the king said.

He took off his ring and put it on Joseph's finger. He hung a great gold chain around Joseph's neck, and gave him a chariot to ride in.

Joseph was the most important man in Egypt, after the king.

That was part of God's plan, too.

The bad years came. In Egypt, food was stored up ready, and no one was hungry. But Joseph's family, back home, had nothing left to eat.

"You must go to Egypt to buy food," Joseph's father said to his brothers.

It was a long, long journey, but they all had to go. Only Ben, the youngest, stayed at home.

"Next time, Ben must come, too," the brothers told Jacob when they got back. "The man in charge says so." They did not know that the man was Joseph.

They often thought about Joseph, and wished they had not been so cruel.

Their father did not want young Ben to go. But in the end he had to. They were all so hungry.

When Joseph saw Ben, he burst into tears.

"It's me, Joseph," he said.

"We're in trouble now," his brothers said to themselves. "Joseph will pay us back for being so unkind to him."

But instead Joseph hugged and kissed them.

"God has taken care of me all this time," he said. "Now *I* will take care of *you*." So the whole family came to Egypt.

10

A Princess and a Baby

"You have a lovely baby boy," said the nurse. The baby waved his little hands and kicked his feet.

His mother held her baby tight and cuddled him close. She should have been so happy—but she was dreadfully afraid.

The people of Israel*–Joseph's family–
had lived in Egypt for a long, long time.
Now they were in danger.

"Kill every baby boy," the cruel king
ordered. "There are too many of these
people in Egypt."

* "Israel" is the special name that was given to Joseph's father,
Jacob.

How could the baby's mother keep him
safe? She must keep him *secret*.

The nurse kept the secret.

Big brother Aaron kept the secret.

Big sister Miriam kept the secret.

The baby slept a lot, and when he cried
his mother quickly hushed him.

But as he grew, the baby made more
noise.

He didn't sleep as much.
He chuckled and laughed.
He bellowed for his dinner.
His mother was *dreadfully* afraid.
Soon someone would find out her secret.

"Go down to the river and get me some reeds," she said to big sister Miriam one day.

"Bring me some sticky tar," she said to big brother Aaron.

Whatever was she doing?

She was making a little basket out of reeds, with tar to keep the water out.

When it was finished, she put the baby inside. Then she hid the basket among the tall reeds at the river's edge.

"You stay here and make sure he's safe," she said to big sister Miriam. Then she went home.

Someone was coming!

It was the king's own daughter.

"Whatever is that?" she said when she saw the basket. She opened the lid–and there was the baby, with tears trickling down his cheeks.

"Poor little thing!" the princess said. "He must be hungry."

"Shall I go and get help?" big sister Miriam offered.

"Yes please," said the princess.

So Miriam ran home to get her mother.

"Look after this baby till he's old enough to come and live with me," the princess said. She was talking to the baby's own mother, though she did not know it. "We shall call him Moses."

11

The King Who Said No

Moses lived in the king's palace.

But he did not belong there. He was one of the people of Israel.

The king of Egypt made the people of Israel his slaves. Men with cruel whips made them work harder and harder.

Moses tried to help, but that only made the king angry.

So Moses ran away, far away, to another land, where he worked as a shepherd.

One day, when he was minding the sheep, he saw something *very* strange.

In the middle of a bush, a fire burned. He could see the flames – but the bush was not burned up.

Moses went closer.

Then he heard a voice, calling his name: "Moses! Moses!"

God was speaking to him.

"I have a special job for you," God
said. "I know all about the cruel king of
Egypt and the horrible things he does.
The people of Israel are *my* people.
Go and tell the king he must let my
people go."

But Moses did not want to.

"I can't do that," he said. "The king of Egypt is very angry with me."

"You can do it if I help you," God said. "Tell my people what I have said. Tell them it's time they had a land of their own. If you are afraid, take Aaron with you."

Moses and Aaron went to see the king.

"God says, 'Let my people go.' "

"God? Who is God? I don't know your God," said the king. And he made the Israelites work harder than ever.

So God sent Moses to warn the king.

"Let my people go, or I will send a terrible disaster. You will have no clean water to drink."

The king said no.
And there *was* no clean water to drink
–just as God said. *Disaster number one.*

Again God sent Moses to warn the king.
"Let my people go, or I will send a
terrible disaster. There will be frogs
everywhere: frogs in the soup, and frogs
in bed with you!"

The king said no.

And there *were* frogs everywhere– hopping and jumping. Frogs in the soup and frogs in people's beds, just as God said. *Disaster number two.*

"Please get rid of these frogs!" begged the king.

The king asked Moses and Moses asked God, and God got rid of the frogs. But the king did not let God's people go.

Again God sent Moses to warn the king.

"Let my people go, or there will be gnats all over the place–nasty little biting gnats."

The king said no.

And there *were* gnats all over the place –nasty little biting gnats–just as God said. *Disaster number three.*

"No! No! No!" shrieked the king, stamping his foot. "I *still* say no."

Then the disasters came thick and fast: *four, five, six, seven, eight, nine… TEN.*

"Yes! Yes! Yes!" groaned the king at last. "Tell God I will let his people go –and good riddance."

If only he had said yes before!

The people of Israel got ready to go.
They were leaving Egypt for ever.
They would never be slaves again.
They were going to a land of their own.
God had set them free.

12
The Big Adventure

There was a great big noisy party.
Everyone sang and danced.
It was the best party ever.

God's people were safe at last –
safe from the king of Egypt.
   "Thank you, thank you, God!"
they sang as they danced.

When they left Egypt, the people had to walk all the way. They took their pots and pans and food and clothes and blankets. They had to carry everything.

All their sheep and goats and cows went too–the big boys and girls took care of them.

"Shoo! Shoo! Hurry, hurry!" they said.

The sheep *would* stop to nibble the grass.
The goats *would* stop to chew the leaves.
The cows *would* stop to drink the water.
"*Hurry, hurry!*"
The little children soon got tired. Their
mothers and fathers had to carry them.
"Hurry, hurry!" they said. "We aren't
safe yet."

And they *weren't* safe yet, for the king
sent his soldiers chasing after them.
　　But God was with his people.
　　God was showing them the way.
　　God was keeping them safe.

They reached the water. It was far too
wide to cross and the soldiers were
catching up with them. What would they
do now?

That night God sent a wind. It blew and blew – and it drove the water away.

Next day the people walked across where the water had been. But God did not let the soldiers follow them.

The people were safe on the other side! That's why they danced and sang.

"Thank you, thank you, *thank you*, God!"

They were going to a land of their own,
the land God promised.
    They were going on a journey:
    a journey through the desert;
    a journey through the mountains;
    a long, hard journey.
    But God was going with them.
God would show them the way.

At night they put up tents to sleep in. Next day they took them down again and moved on.

They had to find food for the animals. They had to find water.

When they found a good place, they put up their tents again. It was hard to keep moving on.

Soon the food ran out and the people were
hungry. They grumbled at Moses.

"We had plenty of food in Egypt," they said.

"God will give you food," Moses answered.

That night a flock of little birds flew in.
They had come a long way. So they were tired
and easy to catch. And the people had meat to
eat.

In the morning the ground was covered with frosty white flakes. They tasted like biscuits made with honey – delicious! The people called this new food "manna".

Soon the water ran out and the people were thirsty. They grumbled at Moses again.

"We had plenty of water in Egypt."

"God will give you water," Moses said.
Then he hit the rock with his stick, and
good fresh water came out.

For every day of the journey, God gave
the people manna to eat.
    For every day of the journey, God
helped the people find water.
    God took care of his people all the
time.

13

The Best Way to Live

Boom! Boom! rolled the thunder.
Zig-zag went the lightning across the sky.
It was very scary.

The people of Israel had reached the great
mountain—the place where God had told
Moses to bring them.

God spoke to Moses, and Moses spoke to the people.

"I love you, and I want you to be my special people," God said. "But first I will tell you the best way to live."

Boom! Boom! rolled the thunder.
Zig-zag went the lightning across the sky.
It was *very* scary.

God spoke to Moses, and Moses told the people the best way to live. He gave them ten good rules to help them be happy:

"One," God said: "Always remember that I am your God. I have rescued you, and I love you.

"Two: Don't let *anything* else take my place.

"Three: Remember who I am when you talk about me.

"Four: There are six days for work and one day for rest—that's my special day.

"Five: Always listen to your mother and father; never make them unhappy.

"Six: You must not take a person's life, for life is very precious.

"Seven: Husbands and wives must keep their special love just for each other.

"Eight: Don't steal what belongs to someone else.

"Nine: Don't tell lies.

"Ten: Don't be greedy for what other people have."

God spoke to Moses and Moses told the people many other things.

"The best way to live," Moses said, at last, "is to love God, and to love one another. This is what God wants. This is the way to be really happy. What do you say?"

"We say, 'Yes—we will love God'," the people promised. "We will live as God wants. That's best. It's the way to be really happy."

So the people of Israel became God's special people.

All that God said about the best way to
live was written down.

"Put a copy in a special box that you
can carry with you," God said. "And
make me a tent of my own. It's to go in
the middle of your camp, to remind you
that I am there with you always."

The people did as God said. They made
the special box. (They called it the Ark,
like Noah's boat.) And they made a most
beautiful tent for God. Everyone gave
their very best things to make it lovely.

Moses' brother, Aaron, was the High
Priest, in charge of everything to do with
God. He had special clothes to wear.

Aaron helped the people keep their
promise to love God and to live as God
wants.

Now it was time to leave the great
mountain. The people took down their
tents, and set out once more.
    They were going on a journey:
    a journey to a land of their own;
    a journey to the land God promised.
    And God was going with them.

14

The Land of the Giants

Joshua and Caleb crept forward.
No one must see them.
They were taking a secret look around
the land – the land God had promised.

Now they could see the valley below.

"Just look at all those grapes," said Joshua.

"The biggest and juiciest I've ever seen," Caleb said. "We must take some back to Moses. This is a *good* land for our people."

Moses had sent twelve men to spy out the
land—north and south and east and west.
Joshua and Caleb came back to Moses.

"It's a *good* land," they said. "Just look
at these grapes!" They were almost too
heavy to carry.
"Let's go there *now*," Caleb said. "We
know God will help us."

But the other spies were much too scared.

"We saw giants in the land," they told Moses.

"We saw *giants* in the land," they said to the people. "They will stamp on us like grasshoppers."

Then all the people were very scared too.
They grumbled and grumbled.

"Why is God taking us to a land of
giants? We want to go back to Egypt."

"It's a *good* land," Joshua and Caleb
said again. "Don't be scared. We know
that God will help us."

But no one would listen.

"Why won't my people trust me?" God said to Moses.

"Didn't I rescue them from Egypt? Didn't I help them find food and water in the desert? Why won't they trust me to help them now? They don't deserve a new land full of good things."

"No," Moses said. "They don't. But I know that you love us, even when we don't deserve it. So won't you give us another chance?"

"Not the grown-ups," God said, "because they would not trust me. Just the children. They will go in and enjoy the new land—when *they* are grown up. Joshua and Caleb too—because they trusted me."

So the people stayed for forty long years in the desert–until the children were grown up. All because they would not trust God to help them.

15

Joshua Wins the Day

"Open up! Open up!
"There are spies in your house.
Bring them out!"

The king's men shouted and banged at
the door of Rahab's house in the city of
Jericho.

Joshua had sent two spies across the
river—the Jordan river—and Rahab had
hidden them.

Rahab didn't want the king's men to find the spies. So she sent them to look somewhere else.

"If you're quick you may catch them," she said, as the soldiers hurried off.

When the king's men had gone, Rahab said to the spies, "God will give you this city. I know it. When that happens, promise you'll be kind to my family, as I have been kind to you."

"We promise," they said.

Joshua was the leader of God's people
now. It was time to go into the promised
land. God was going with them, to help
them.

"Tomorrow we cross the river–the
Jordan river," Joshua said. The Jordan
river was deep and wide, but Joshua
trusted God.

The people had come to the end of their
long, long journey.

They still had to cross the deep, wide
river—but God would help them.

The men who carried the Ark went
first. They stepped into the river…

…and at that very moment the water stopped coming!

They stood in the middle of the deep wide river which was quite dried up, and the people went safely across.

Now they *knew* that God was going with them. They trusted God and were *not* afraid.

The big wooden gates of the city of Jericho were shut tight. The people inside *were* afraid.

Outside, the soldiers of Israel marched around the walls: once around the walls. They didn't talk. They didn't shout.

In front went the men with the trumpets:

TARAA! TARARAA!

Every day, for six days, the soldiers marched around the walls: once around the walls. They didn't talk. They didn't shout.

Every day, for six days, the men with the trumpets went in front:

TARAA! TARARAA!

The seventh day came. The soldiers
marched around the walls…
and around the walls
and around the walls
seven times around the walls.

Then the men with the trumpets lifted
them high… and *blew*:
TARAA! TARARAA!
And the soldiers all SHOUTED!

"God has given us the city!" Joshua
cried.
    Then the walls began to shake.
    The walls began to crack.
    The walls began to crumble…

…And with a great C-R-A-S-H! the walls
fell down.
    God had given them the city.

16

Farmer Gideon's Men

The people of Israel were hiding. They hid in caves. They hid in the hills. They were hiding from the Men on Camels.*

The Men on Camels came riding into the promised land from beyond the river–the Jordan river. They took away the sheep. They took away the cows. They took away the donkeys. They trampled on the corn as soon as it was planted.

*The Midianites.

Why did God let them?

God still loved the people of Israel, but they had broken their promise to love him and to live as he wants.

The people of Israel had no wool. They had no milk. They had no bread. They were afraid of the Men on Camels—there were too many of them to count.

"Help! Help! Please help us," they
cried to God.

And God answered them.

"You have broken your promise,"
God said. "Yet now that you are in
trouble you want me to help. And I *will*
help–because I still love you."

God went to find Farmer Gideon.

"I have a special job for you," God said. "You must rescue my people from those Men on Camels."

"But I can't fight them," Farmer Gideon objected. "I'm a farmer, not a soldier."

"You can if I help you," God said.

The Men on Camels came riding in again
from beyond the river – the Jordan river
– too many of them to count.

Then Farmer Gideon blew a long blast
on his trumpet:

TAN TAN TARAA!

He was calling for help – and the men
came running.

"Too many," God said. "Tell the ones
who are scared to go home."

"Still too many," God said, as Gideon watched them go. "Take the ones who are left to the stream to drink. The ones I want will cup their hands and lap like dogs. That way, they can keep a look-out for danger. The rest can go home."

That left just 300 to fight the Men on Camels, who were too many to count.

That night, God said to Gideon: "Get up! It's time to go."

Gideon gave every man a trumpet. He gave every man a flaming torch and a jar to hide it in.

All was quiet.

They crept up close to the Men on Camels, who were still fast asleep! Now Gideon's men were all around their camp.

TARAA! TARAA! TARARAAA!

What was that terrible noise in the quiet night? Gideon's men were blowing their trumpets! What was that blaze of light in the dark? Gideon's men had broken the jars that hid their flaming torches!

The Men on Camels woke up in a fright. They were *so* scared that they leapt on their camels and fled.

17

The Lion-Killer

Samson was different from all the other boys. His dark curly hair grew down past his shoulders. And Samson was STRONG–stronger than any other boy.

It was God who made Samson strong. It was God who said Samson's hair must never be cut. It was the sign that Samson was *God's* strong man.*

* This was a rule for people specially dedicated to God, who took the "Nazirite" vow.

One day, when Samson was out for a walk, he heard a great *roar*.

It was a lion—a fierce wild lion.

That lion might hurt someone. So Samson went looking for it.

When he found the lion, Samson killed it with his own two hands. God had made him *so* strong.

The people of Israel were in trouble. The People from the Sea* came sailing in and built cities of their own in the promised land. They made God's people very unhappy.

"Help! Help! Please help us," they cried to God.

* The Philistines.

"What about your promise?" God said
to them. "You have broken your promise
to love me and live as I want–yet now
you are in trouble you want me to help.
And I *will* help–because I still love you!"

God chose Samson to rescue them: that
was why God had made him *so* strong.

Samson was grown up now. His hair had never been cut. It was the sign that Samson was *God's* strong man.

He began to make trouble for the People from the Sea. He wasn't a bit afraid of them.

Samson was so strong that when they tied him up, he broke the ropes. When they shut him in, he tore down the doors and carried them off!

Samson made BIG trouble for the People from the Sea, though they tried and tried to catch him.

"What makes you so strong?" asked beautiful Delilah, one day. "You can tell me your secret. I won't tell anyone."

Delilah was helping the People from the Sea to catch Samson. She asked and asked, till at last he said:

"I won't be strong if my hair is cut."

Then the People from the Sea came and cut his hair.

Samson was not God's strong man any more. They put him in prison.

But Samson told God how sorry he was, and God made Samson strong again.
   One last time, Samson made trouble for the People from the Sea: BIG, BIG trouble! He pulled a huge building down, on top of himself and all the people inside.

18

Ruth's New Family

There was no food left at home in Bethlehem, so Naomi and her family went away – to a land that had plenty of food. They stayed away for a long time.

"I must go home again," Naomi decided one day.

She was all alone now: no husband and no children. Her husband and both her boys had died.

"I will go with you," said Orpah, who had married one of Naomi's boys.

"Let me come too," said Ruth, who had married the other. They were kind girls, and they both loved Naomi dearly.

So they set out together. But on the way, Naomi said:

"It was kind of you to come so far. Now you must go back."

The girls both cried. They loved Naomi dearly, and they did not want to leave her. Sadly, Orpah went back.

But Ruth held Naomi tight.

"Let me go with you to Bethlehem," she said. "From now on, your home will be my home; your people will be my people; your God will be my God."

Ruth would not change her mind, so they went on together.

When they got to Bethlehem, everyone was *very* excited.

"Naomi! Is it really you? After all this time?" And they all talked about Ruth.

"How kind she is to Naomi," they said.

It was harvest time in Bethlehem: they were cutting the corn.

Naomi and Ruth were very poor. They had no farm of their own, and no one to help them.

Ruth went out to the fields each day. She picked up the corn that was left, to make bread for them both to eat.

The fields belonged to Farmer Boaz. He saw how hard Ruth worked. He heard how kind she was. And Naomi was one of his family.

"Leave plenty for Ruth," he told his men.

"Wherever did you get all that corn?"
asked Naomi, when Ruth got home.

Ruth told her, and Naomi thought of
a plan. Kind Ruth deserved a good
husband. Farmer Boaz was just the man!

Naomi's plan worked. Ruth and
Farmer Boaz were married. They had a
baby boy. Grannie Naomi was *so* pleased.
She jigged the baby on her knee and they
laughed together.

"Thank you, God, for making me happy again," she said. "And for giving my kind Ruth a family of her own."

One day, when Ruth's baby was grown up, he had a little grandson of his own. *That* baby's name was David–and David became a great king. But that is another story.*

* You will find the stories of David on pages 188-221.

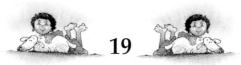

19

One Dark Night

"I do so want a baby," Hannah sobbed. She had wanted a baby of her very own for such a long time. Now she was in the tent of God, telling God all about it. Old Eli, the priest of God, sat listening.

"My baby will always belong to you too," Hannah said to God, "if only you will help me."

God comforted Hannah, and answered her prayer.

Soon she had a baby boy of her very own. She called him Samuel, and she loved him very much.

But she did not forget that her little Sam belonged to God too. As soon as he was old enough, Hannah took Samuel to old Eli, the priest of God.

"Eli will teach Sam to love God and to live as God wants," Hannah said to herself.

Samuel cried a bit, but Eli held his hand kindly.

"Please take good care of him for me," said Hannah. Then, before she went home, she said a special thank-you prayer to God:

"Dear God, you have made me so happy.
There is no one like you.
You know everything.
You give people children
when they have none.
You give food to the hungry.
You take care of the poor.
You keep your people safe."

Eli was kind to Samuel. His own boys were grown up now, but they gave him a lot of trouble. Samuel was no trouble at all. He was quick to learn everything that Eli taught him.

One night, in bed, Samuel heard someone call his name. He got up and ran to Eli.

"Here I am," he said.

"I didn't call you, Sam. Go back to bed."

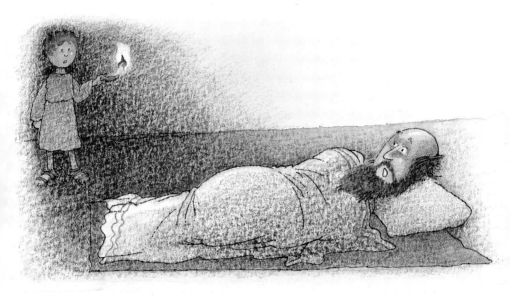

It happened again.

"Here I am."

"I didn't call you, Sam. Go back to bed."

It happened a third time.
"Here I am."

"It's God who wants to speak to you,
Sam," old Eli said then. "Go back to bed.
And next time he calls, tell him you are
listening."

God called again: "Samuel! Samuel!"
  "I'm listening," Samuel said.

God talked to Samuel a lot after that.
Samuel listened to God—and when he
grew up, everyone listened to *him*. They
knew he would tell them what God said.

20

The King Who Was Shy

"We want a king! Give us a king!" the
people shouted.

Samuel sighed. For years and years
now he had taught the people of Israel to
love God and to live as God wants. Why
did they want a king, when they had God?

"A king will be bad for you," Samuel said. "He will take your boys to be his soldiers, and you will be his slaves."

But the people went on shouting, "We want a king! Give us a king!"

"They don't want me any more,"
Samuel said sadly to God.
"It's *me* they don't want," God said.
"After all I've done for them." God was
sad too. But he said to Samuel: "If they
want a king, they shall have a king.
I know just the person."

Saul was tall–much taller than anyone else. He was handsome, too.

One day, his father's donkeys got lost and Saul went looking for them. He could not find them anywhere. So he decided to ask Samuel to help.

As soon as Samuel saw Saul, he said to himself: "This is the man God has chosen to be king."

Saul stayed the night at Samuel's house. Next morning, Samuel broke the news:

"Saul, God has chosen you to be the king of Israel."

"Me? But there's nothing special about me," Saul said in amazement.

"Don't worry," said Samuel. "God is going to help you. Oh, and by the way, the donkeys are safe back home."

Samuel called all the people together.

"God is going to choose you a king," he said. "Let's see which family-tribe he chooses." Everyone belonged to one of the twelve big family-tribes of Israel named after the sons of Jacob.

Samuel counted them—one, two, three… The family-tribe of Benjamin stepped forward.

That was the one.

"Now all the Benjamin families," Samuel said. "One at a time."

He counted them—one, two three… Samuel came to Saul's father.

"God has chosen a king from *this* family," Samuel said.

But where was Saul? He was feeling very shy!

"Look over there," God told them.
"He's hiding behind those sacks of corn."
Saul stood up–and the people saw that
he was tall–much taller than anyone else.
They saw that he was handsome, too.
And they were pleased.
"Here is your king," Samuel told them.
Then everyone clapped and shouted:
"Long live the king!
Long live King Saul!"

21

David and the Giant

David was minding the sheep. He kept a careful eye on them. They must not wander off. No fierce wild animal must hurt them.

David was a shepherd-boy. He was good at his job. The sheep knew they were safe when David was minding them. He found them fields of juicy green grass. He led them to clear fresh water.

David was trying out a new song on his harp–it was fun to make up new songs. What David liked best was making up songs about God. He sang God thanking songs and praising songs and asking songs. David loved God.

His new song went like this:

"God is my shepherd,
so I have everything I need.
He finds me fields of juicy green grass.
He leads me to clear fresh water.
He guides me on the right paths.
Even when it's dark, I need not be afraid,
because God is with me,
keeping me safe.
God is my good shepherd."

"David! David!" One of his brothers came running up the hill. (David had seven big brothers.) "Go home at once. Samuel wants to see you."

God had sent Samuel to David's house to choose the next king. God was not pleased with King Saul. The next king must be someone who loved and trusted God—and God had chosen David!

The People from the Sea picked a fight with King Saul and his soldiers. They had a HUGE man–the giant Goliath–on their side, so they were sure to win.

Goliath was simply ENORMOUS. He was like an iron man: no one could hurt him.

"I dare you, I dare you to fight me," he shouted to King Saul's soldiers. "I dare *anyone* to fight me."

Everyone was scared of this huge iron
man, so no one would fight him.

Every morning and every evening
Goliath stood there shouting, "I dare you,
I dare you to fight me. I dare *anyone* to
fight me!"

But no one did.

They were far too scared.

Three of David's big brothers were among those soldiers.

"Go and see how they are," David's father said to him, one day. "They may be hungry. Here are ten loaves of bread and ten cream-cheeses. And take them some roasted corn—all you can carry."

David got there just in time to hear Goliath shouting, "I dare you, I dare you to fight me. I dare *anyone* to fight me!"

When no one moved, David talked to the soldiers.

"That giant's too big for his boots! We shouldn't let him get away with it. This is *God's* army!"

"You're the one who's too big for his boots," his brothers said crossly.

King Saul sent for David.

"*I'm* not scared," David said. "*I'll* fight him!"

"But you're only a boy," said the king.

"I mind the sheep at home," David said. "Sometimes lions and bears try to snatch a lamb, and I have to kill them. If God can keep me safe from lions and bears, he can keep me safe from this giant."

The king dressed David up as a soldier.
But everything was far too big.

He gave David his own sword. But it
was far too heavy.

"I can't wear all this to fight the giant,"
David said, as he put his own clothes on
again. "I can hardly walk!"

David took his strong stick and went down to the stream. He chose five smooth stones to fit his shepherd's sling. Then he went to fight the giant.

"What's *this*?" the giant roared. "A boy with a stick, come to fight ME?"

"God doesn't need big men with swords to save his people," David answered.

He took one of the five smooth stones,
and fired it from his sling:
     WHIZZZ!

The stone hit Goliath right on the
forehead and knocked him flat. David cut
off Goliath's head with the giant's own
sword.
    King Saul's army cheered and cheered
–and the People from the Sea all ran
away!

22

Best Friends

David came to stay at the palace after he killed the giant.

King Saul had a son–Prince Jonathan. Jonathan was brave, and he was kind.

As soon as they met, Jonathan and David were friends, best friends. They promised to be best friends for ever.

King Saul had bad moods and David
cheered him up. Every day, David played
his harp and sang for the king.

"Be full of joy.
Sing happy songs!
Never forget that the Lord God made us.
We belong to him.
We are his people.
God is good, and he loves us for ever."

Suddenly, the king threw his spear at David–he only just escaped!

The king was jealous of David.

David was a hero because he had killed Goliath. People loved David more than they loved King Saul.

King Saul was *so* jealous, he wanted to hurt David. Jonathan was worried.

"Why do you want to hurt my friend David?" Jonathan asked his father. "Didn't he fight Goliath for you? He might have been killed."

The king was ashamed of himself.

"You are right," he said. "I won't hurt David. I promise."

But one day King Saul threw his spear at David *again*. That night David escaped from the palace.

David's place at the table was empty.

"Where is he?" asked the king.

"He's gone away," said Jonathan.

King Saul did not like Jonathan taking sides with David. He flew into a rage.

Jonathan went to the friends' secret meeting-place.

"The king really means to hurt you," he said to David. "You must go right away. It's not safe to come back."

They hugged and cried as they said goodbye. They could not be together now. But they were still best friends, and they stayed best friends for ever.

23

The Outlaw

God had chosen David to be king after Saul. King Saul tried to hurt David. But David would never hurt King Saul.

The king sent his soldiers to find David. David and his men had to hide from them.

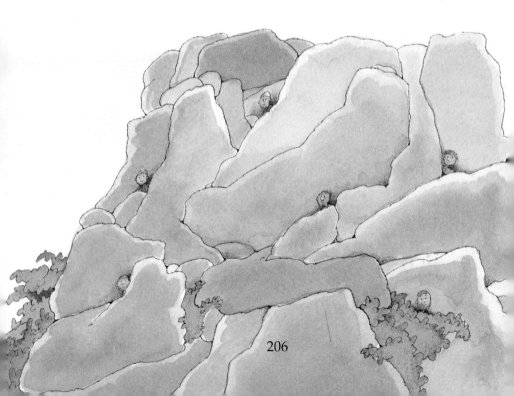

Once, they hid in a cave. They crouched
down right at the back, in the dark.

    King Saul came into the cave and sat
down. He did not see them.

Softly, softly, David crept up close.

The king did not hear him.

David drew his sword and cut off the edge of Saul's cloak.

The king did not see him.

The king went away—and David came
out of the cave.

"See this?" David shouted after him.
"I drew my sword and cut off the edge of
your cloak. But I didn't hurt *you*: I will
never hurt *you*. So why do you want to
hurt me?"

King Saul was ashamed of himself.

"I have been very wrong," he said.
And he took his soldiers away.

But soon they were hunting for David
again. One night, when King Saul and his
soldiers were all fast asleep, David crept
up close.

The king did not hear him.

David seized the king's spear and the
water jar right by his head.

The king did not see him.

David got safely away. Then he shouted
to the king:

"Can you hear me? I have taken your
spear, and the water jar right by your
head. But I didn't hurt *you*: I will *never*
hurt *you*. So why do you want to hurt
me?"

King Saul was ashamed of himself.

"I have been very wrong," he said.
And again he took his soldiers away.

The People from the Sea came to fight the people of Israel. There was a fierce battle. King Saul and Jonathan were killed.

David was very sad when he heard the news. He had never hurt King Saul, though the king was unkind to him. And Jonathan was David's best friend.

David put all his sadness into a special song:

"Swifter than eagles
stronger than lions
were Saul and Jonathan.
The brave soldiers have fallen
–they were killed in battle.
How sad I am for you, Jonathan.
How much I will miss you–
the best of all best friends."

David was sad–but now it was safe to
come home. He was king at last. God had
kept his promise.

24

King David's Great Idea

King David had his own fine house in the
city of Jerusalem.

One day, he had a great idea.

"God ought to have a new house, too.
I will build God a beautiful temple."

He couldn't wait to begin, he was so
excited.

But God said, "No. One of your sons will
build my temple—but not you."

David was very disappointed. But God
had a special promise for him.

"I will make you a great and famous
king," God said, "and your family will be
kings for ever."

God always keeps his promises.

David *was* a great and famous king.
He won many battles, and he kept his
people safe. But he never stopped
thinking about that temple for God.

King David thought of a plan. He couldn't build the temple, but he *could* get things ready. That was a great idea!

He made himself a list.
　　"One: we'll need stones, *big* stones."
　　So they brought big stones, piles of big stones, to build God's temple.

"Two: we'll need wood – the *best* wood."

So they brought the best wood, stacks of beautiful cedar wood, to build God's temple.

"Three: we'll need iron.

"Four: we'll need bronze.

"Five and six and seven: we'll need gold and silver and jewels…"

So they brought mountains of iron and bronze. They brought chests full of gold and silver and jewels. All to build God's temple.

"I think that's everything," David said at last. "Now for the people to do the work." And he made another list.

"One: we'll need people to look after God's temple. That's your job," he said to the family of Levi.

"Two: we'll need people to help us come to God. That's *your* job," he said to the priests.

"Now for the music. This will be *fun*! We'll need harps to play the tunes, cymbals to make a loud noise—and the best singers we can find for the choir."

David wrote some of his own special
songs–psalms to sing in God's temple.
The choir made up new songs too.

"Praise God in his temple!
Praise God with trumpets.
   TAN TAN TARAA!
Praise God with harps.
Praise God with drums and dancing.
   BOUM-DI-BOUM!
   BOUM-DIDI-BOUM!
Praise God with LOUD cymbals!
Praise God, everyone!"

Now everything was ready. David was
very happy.

"Thank you, God," he said, "for
everything you give us. Oh, and when
the time comes, please help my son
Solomon to build your temple."

25

Solomon the Magnificent

Solomon was king now. Like his father King David, Solomon loved God. One night when he was fast asleep, King Solomon had a dream.

"What would you like me to give you?" God asked him in his dream.

Solomon could have anything he wanted. He could be rich. He could be famous.

How hard it was to choose!

"I want to be a good king," he said at last. "One who is always fair. I can't be fair unless I am wise—so please make me wise."

It was a good answer.

"You *shall* be wise," God said, "the wisest king in the world. And I will make you rich and famous too."

Kings and queens came to hear King Solomon's wise words. He knew all about trees and plants, about birds and animals *–and* about people too.

Everyone wanted to remember Solomon's proverbs, so they wrote his wise words down:

"Do what is right and fair, if you want to please God."

"Kind words are as sweet as honey."

"It's good to take care of animals."

"A smile makes you feel happy."

King Solomon was wise–*and* he was rich and famous.

King Solomon was going to build the temple for God. Everything was ready.

His father, King David, had gathered together the piles of stones and stacks of wood; the mountains of iron and bronze; the chests full of silver and gold and jewels—all ready to build.

"Let's get started!" King Solomon said to his workers.

"You must cut the stones."

Chip. Chip. Hammer. Hammer.

"You must carve the wood."
"You must melt the gold."

The workers did as King Solomon said.
They all did their very best for the
temple of God. It was *so* beautiful.

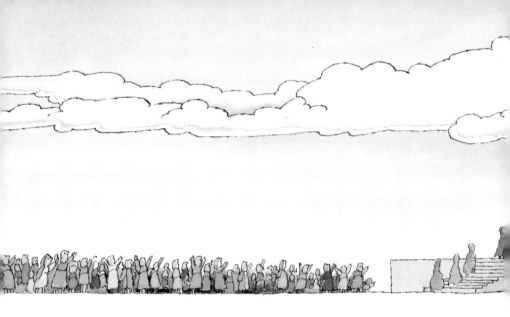

At last the temple was finished. All was ready for the grand opening.

The king was there—and all the workers; and all the people; the family of Levi who looked after the temple; the priests who helped the people come to God; the choir and the band.

It was a *very* special occasion.

The Ark had a place of its own in the
temple. The Ark was the special box
where they kept the copy of God's good
rules for the best way to live.

The trumpets blew:
    TARAA! TARARAA!
    CRASH! CRASH! went the cymbals.
And the people sang at the tops of their
voices:
    "God is good. God's love is for ever!"

Then King Solomon spoke out loud to God:

"You are the one who made the whole world," he said. "We know you can't really live in a house, like us. But we want your temple to be a very special place: a place where we can come to you; a special place to say our prayers."

King Solomon spoke to the excited
people.

"God bless you and make you happy!"
he said. "And now–let the fun begin!"

The party went on and on. It was
seven whole days before the people went
home, tired but still happy.

26

A Very Hungry Time

Bad King Ahab and wicked Queen Jezebel did not love God, or take good care of his people.

God's people were in trouble. King Solomon had died long ago. His great kingdom now had two kings. One king ruled in the north (that was King Ahab). Another king ruled in the south (he was one of King David's family).

King Ahab built a temple. It wasn't God's temple. Inside was a block of stone, with the picture of a man on it. Queen Jezebel and her people called the man Baal, as if he were real.

"Baal, please make it rain," they said to him. Or "Baal, please don't send a storm."

But Baal was only a picture on a block of stone. He wasn't alive. He couldn't really do anything.

Elijah the prophet went to King Ahab
with a message from God. A prophet is
someone who brings special messages
from God.

"You think that Baal knows all about
the weather," Elijah said. "He doesn't
—but God does. And God says this: 'It's
going to stay dry—no rain at all, until I
say so.' Just you wait and see."

King Ahab did not believe it.

But all that day the sun shone.
Every day, day after day, the sun shone.
The days and the weeks and the months
went by. Not a drop of rain.
   Everyone began to get worried.
   No rain means nothing will grow.
   No rain means no water to drink.

All day, every day, the sun shone.

The plants began to droop and die: soon there would be nothing to eat.

The rivers began to dry up: soon there would be nothing to drink.

"Where is Elijah?" roared the king. "Just let me get my hands on him!"

But no one knew where Elijah was— no one but God.

Elijah was down by the brook.
There was still some water to drink,
and he had food to eat. God was looking
after Elijah and keeping him safe.
Still the sun shone…

…And Elijah's brook dried up. Where
would he go now?

"I'll tell you where to go," God said. So Elijah set off.

He was almost there when he met a poor woman, picking up sticks for her fire.

"I'm very thirsty," Elijah said – and she went to fetch him some water. "I'm hungry too," Elijah called after her.

"We have nothing left but a handful of flour and a drop of oil," she said sadly. "And my little boy is *so* hungry."

"Don't worry," Elijah said. "Bake *me* a loaf first and then bake your own. You won't go hungry. Your flour and your oil will last till the rain comes. God himself says so."

So she did as Elijah said…

…And there was bread to eat, every day. Bread for Elijah, and the woman, and her son. Because God was looking after them.

27

Elijah's Big Day

There had been no rain for a very long time. The king blamed Elijah. He was so angry he wanted to kill him. But he couldn't find Elijah anywhere, because God was keeping him safe.

King Ahab did not care that his people were hungry and thirsty. But God did.

"Go to see the king," God said to Elijah, "and I will send rain."

"Here comes trouble," growled the king, as soon as he saw Elijah.

"If you would only listen to God instead of that block of stone you call Baal, there would *be* no trouble," said Elijah. "Now, get everyone together–and we'll see which is the *real* God."

"You can't have God *and* Baal," Elijah said to the people. "You must choose between them. We'll see which is the *real* God.

"Let's make two piles of stone, one for Baal and one for God. We'll put wood on top of the stones, and meat on top of the wood. The *real* God is the one who can light the fire to cook the meat."

"Yes! Yes!" the people shouted. "The *real* God is the one who lights the fire!"

"You first," Elijah said to Baal's people. So they made their pile of stones. They put wood on top of the stones, and meat on top of the wood. Then they asked Baal to light the fire.

But nothing happened.

Round and round their pile of stones
they danced, shouting: "Answer us, Baal.
Answer us, Baal."
But still nothing happened.

Elijah began to tease them.

"Shout a bit louder–perhaps Baal is asleep!"

Baal's people danced and danced till they were worn out. They screamed and shouted till they were hoarse.

But still nothing happened.

"It's my turn now," Elijah said, and everyone gathered round to watch.

Elijah made his pile of twelve big stones.
He put wood on top of the stones, and
meat on top of the wood. And he made
the people pour water all over it!

Then Elijah talked to God. He didn't
shout. He didn't dance. He didn't need to
–he knew that God was listening.

"Let all the people see that *you* are the
real God," Elijah said.

At that very moment the fire came.

It burned the wet wood; it roasted the wet meat—what a *delicious* smell!
    The people all bowed to the ground: "This is the *real* God," they cried, "the *only* real God."

Then at last God sent the rain.
    The hungry, thirsty time was over.

28

The Girl Who Helped

General Naaman looked at himself in the
mirror. He had spots and sore places all
over!

"It's getting worse," he said gloomily.

His wife gave a sigh. They were *very*
worried. But what could they do? Not
even the cleverest doctor could help.

General Naaman had led his army into battle against the people of Israel – and won. He brought a little girl home to help his wife.

The girl was very unhappy. She missed her mother and father, her brothers and her sisters *so* much. But Mrs Naaman was kind. She dried the girl's tears.

Now the little girl wanted to help them.
"There's a man back home in Israel
who can make people better," she said.
Mrs Naaman told the General.⁻
And General Naaman told the king.
The king wrote a letter–at once–and
the General set off, with his horses and
his men.

The king of Israel read the letter.

"My General is ill," it said. "I want you to make him better."

"I can't make people better," the king of Israel said. "But if I don't, there will be another battle. Whatever shall I do?"

"Just send him to me," said the prophet Elisha.* "God can make him well."

* After Elijah, Elisha became God's prophet.

So General Naaman went to see Elisha.
   But Elisha didn't even come to the
door. He just sent a message:
   "Wash seven times in the river–the
Jordan river–and you will be well again."

The General rode off in a huff. He wasn't going to do as Elisha said.

"The man didn't even come to the door! And if all I have to do is wash, there are nicer rivers at home!"

"But it's such an *easy* thing to do," his men said. "Why not just try it?"

So General Naaman went to the river –the Jordan river.

He washed himself once. He washed
himself twice. He washed himself three
times.

He washed himself four, five, six times.
He washed himself SEVEN times…

…Then he looked at his arms—no spots or sore places there. He looked at his legs—no spots or sore places there. Not a spot, not a sore place *anywhere*!

He was well again!

Hooray for Elisha. Hooray for God.
And hooray for the girl who helped.

29

A Very Scary Time

"The soldiers are coming! The enemy soldiers are coming! Run! Run!"

As soon as they heard it, they ran for their lives. Mothers and fathers and children all ran to the city. The city of Jerusalem had big thick walls all around it. The city of Jerusalem had big strong gates.

They hurried inside–only just in time.

"Shut the gates!" cried the king of Jerusalem. And the big strong gates of the city were shut tight.

Everyone was safe inside. The cruel enemy soldiers* could not get in.

* The army of Assyria, the big power in the north.

"Let us in! Let us in!" the soldiers
shouted.

But the king of Jerusalem would *not* let
them in.

"Let us in! Let us in!" the soldiers
shouted. "Don't expect God to help you.
All the other cities have let us in."

But the king of Jerusalem would *not* let them in. He trusted God. He knew that God *would* help his people.

No food came into the city.

The mothers and fathers and children were hungry. That made the king very sad.

There was a prophet in the city of
Jerusalem who brought God's messages
to the people. His name was Isaiah.

"God says the enemy soldiers will *not*
get in," Isaiah said to the king. "God *will*
help us. He's going to send them all
away."

The king of Jerusalem went to the temple for a special talk with God.

"Lord God," he said, "you made the whole world and everything in it. Nothing is too hard for you. Please help us. Show those enemy soldiers that you are the one who is really in charge."

The king of Jerusalem trusted God.
The prophet Isaiah trusted God.
And God *did* help his people.

The very next day, when the mothers and
fathers and children peeped out from the
city walls…

…the enemy soldiers were marching off!
God had sent them all away.

"Open the gates!" cried the king of Jerusalem. And the big strong gates of the city were opened wide. It was safe for the mothers and fathers and children to go home.

"Three cheers for the king! Three cheers for the prophet Isaiah!" they shouted. "And hip, hip hooray for God, who has kept us all safe!"

30

A Fishy Story

Jonah was running away. He was running away to sea.

"Go to Nineveh,"* God said to Jonah. "The people there are doing wicked things. Tell them to stop being nasty at once, or there will be trouble."

Jonah did not want to do as God told him—so he ran away from God.

* The capital city of enemy Assyria.

The people of Nineveh were the fierce enemies of Jonah's people, the people of Israel. Jonah wanted God to punish them.

If he went to warn them, they might stop being nasty. Then God would be kind to them.

Jonah did not want that. That was why he was running away.

The ship sailed away with Jonah on board.

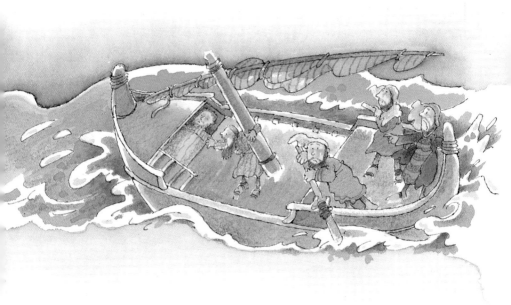

He was so tired, he fell fast asleep. He was *so* tired he didn't hear the wind blow, stronger and stronger. He didn't feel the waves rock and toss and throw the ship about. He didn't hear the sailors' frightened cries.

He did not know there was a storm – a very scary storm.

"Wake up! Wake up!" said the captain, shaking Jonah hard. "Say your prayers, before we all drown!"

But Jonah was running away from God. How could he ask God to help him?

"It's all my fault," Jonah said to the sailors. "You must throw me into the sea."

No one wanted to do that, but in the end they did. And at once the sea was calm.

Down, down, down Jonah sank. Deep down, beneath the waves. But God did not let him drown. God sent a great big fish, and…

GULP! GULP! GULP!

…Jonah was safe inside. It was dark and slippy and slimy in there. But Jonah was alive!

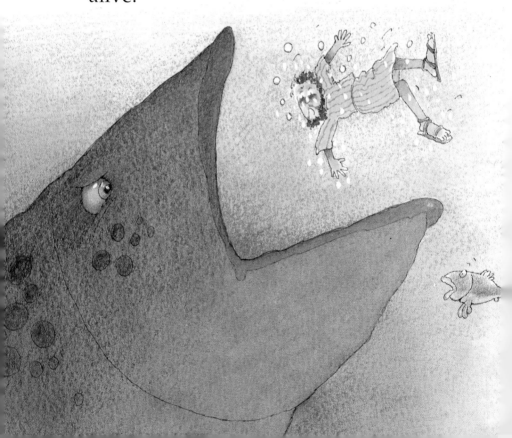

"You saved my life," Jonah said to God. "Thank you. I'm sorry I ran away. Next time I'll do as you tell me—if I ever get out!"

Jonah was stuck inside the fish for three whole days. Then…

HIC! HIC! HICCUP!

…the fish spat Jonah out on a nice dry beach.

Jonah took a BIG breath of fresh air.
He held his face up to the warm sun.
He wriggled his toes in the soft sand –
and then he set off.

"God is going to *punish* you," Jonah
told the people of Nineveh. "He knows
all about you – every nasty little thing!"

Then the people of Nineveh were sorry.
They stopped being nasty – and God was
kind to them.

Jonah sat in the hot sun and sulked. He was *very* cross.

"I just knew this would happen," he grumbled to God. "I wanted you to *punish* those people! They are our enemies–they *deserved* to be punished!"

But God said: "Think of all those children, and the animals too. I love *everyone*–yes, even the people of Nineveh. Isn't that a good thing?"

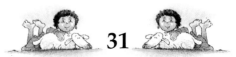

31

When the Lions Roared

Daniel was far away from his home in Jerusalem. He had been taken prisoner. But even in far-away Babylon, Daniel trusted God and did as God said.

Every day he prayed to God. And God made Daniel wise—the wisest of all the wise men of Babylon.

One day, the king chose Daniel for a very important job. That made all the other wise men jealous—they wanted to get rid of him.

But Daniel was brave: they couldn't scare him. And he never did anything bad or nasty—so they couldn't tell tales to the king.

How *could* they get rid of him? They thought and thought. Then one of them had a clever idea.

"Daniel wants to please God even more than he wants to please the king. So this is what we'll do…"

Whisper, whisper, whisper.

The wise men of Babylon went to the king.

"O king, live for ever," they said, bowing low. "We want you to make a new law. Tell everyone they must pray to you only—or be thrown to the lions!"

The king did not know it was all a trick to get rid of Daniel. So he made the new law—a law that could not be changed.

Daniel soon knew about the king's new law—everyone did. But he wanted to please God even more than he wanted to please the king. So he prayed to God, as he always did.

The wise men of Babylon saw him, kneeling at his window. Their plan had worked. Chuckling with glee, they hurried to tell the king.

"O king, live for ever," they said, bowing low and pretending to feel sad. "We bring bad news. Daniel has disobeyed your new law. We saw him ourselves, praying to God at his window. The law is clear. Daniel must be thrown to the lions."

The king was *most* upset. But the law could not be changed. He could not save Daniel.

The lions were hungry.
   They ROARED for their supper.

   "I do hope God can save you," the
king said to Daniel, as they pushed him
in with the lions and fastened the door.
   All night long the king lay awake,
thinking about Daniel–and those hungry
roaring lions.

As soon as it was light, he hurried back.
The door was still shut tight. Everything
was quiet.

"Daniel! Daniel!" the king called
anxiously. "Has God been able to save
you from the lions?" He felt sure those
hungry lions had eaten Daniel for their
supper.

But Daniel's voice came back, loud and clear.

"O king, live for ever–yes, he has! The lions haven't opened their mouths all night. I am quite safe–not a scratch on me!"

The king gave a great whoop of joy!

"Let him out. AT ONCE!" he ordered.

Daniel came out. He wasn't hurt at all. God had saved him from the lions.

32

A New King

"Trouble, trouble—we're always in trouble. God must have forgotten all about us," the people said. "Will the trouble never end?"

"One day, some day, it will," said the prophet Isaiah. "God has not forgotten you. He has given me a special message for you. Just listen to this:

'When everything seems dark
you will see a shining light.
A child will be born
—a new king for my people.
"Wise Counsellor" he will be called,
and "Prince of Peace".
He will be just and fair.
There will be peace in his kingdom for ever
  and ever.
One day—just you wait and see.

'One day, some day,
all the hurting will stop.
You will all know me
and I will never leave you.
The wolf will not hurt the sheep.
The calf and the baby bear
will go to sleep together
–and little children will take care of them.
One day, some day–just you wait and see.'"

So the people were comforted in their trouble.

"God has not forgotten us," they said. "We will wait for the new king God has promised to send. He will make everything all right. We hope he will come soon."

New Testament Stories

33

Mary and the Angel

Mary sang a little song to herself as she swept and tidied the house in Nazareth.* She was *so* happy.

She was thinking about her wedding day. Mary was going to marry Joseph.

"How kind he is," she thought. "And how clever at making things." Joseph made doors. He made tables and chairs. He was a carpenter.

* A small town in the north of present-day Israel.

Mary was so busy with her thoughts that she jumped when she heard the voice.

She turned to look…

…and her eyes grew round with surprise. For there, by the door, stood a shining angel!

Mary knew about angels: God sent them
when he had something special to say.
But she had never expected to see one.

Angel Gabriel stood there a moment.
He did not want to frighten her.

"I bring good news, Mary," the angel said, gently. "God has a wonderful plan for you. You are going to have a baby – a very special baby. His name is Jesus. He will be God's promised King. God himself will be his father."

"But I don't understand…" Mary said.

"God will take care of everything," said Angel Gabriel. "Nothing is too hard for him.

"Everyone thought that Cousin Elizabeth would never have a baby. But she will, very soon. Her baby, too, is part of God's plan."

Mary's eyes opened wide in wonder.

"I shall be *glad* to do whatever God wants," she said softly.

Then, as swiftly as he had come, Angel Gabriel was gone. Mary rubbed her eyes. Had she *really* been talking to an angel?

She was bursting to tell someone.

"I'll go to see Elizabeth," Mary said. "She's sure to understand."

"Zechariah* saw an angel too,"
Elizabeth said, when Mary had unpacked
and they were sitting down together. "He
came to tell us about *our* baby. And now
God has chosen *you* to be the mother of
the promised King!"

Suddenly, Mary felt all bubbly with
joy—*so* happy that she began to sing…

* Elizabeth's husband: this story is told in Luke chapter 1.

"Dear God,
how great you are!
How glad you make me.
Everyone will know
how you have blessed* me
–though I am no one special.
For you have done great things for me…
You have come to help your people
as you promised long ago."**

After her visit, Mary went home. God
told Joseph all about Mary's special baby.
And soon they were married.

* When God "blesses" someone he makes something good happen.
** Page 281 tells of this promise.

34

The Very Special Baby

In the far-away city of Rome, Emperor Augustus needed money.

"Write down the names of all the people in every country that I rule," he said. "I want to make sure they pay my tax."

The Emperor's order went out, away across the sea, to the far-off land where Mary and Joseph lived.*

---

* This was the time of the Roman Empire, when the Jewish people were under Roman rule.

"We must go to Bethlehem," Joseph said, "to put our names on the Emperor's list."

It was a long way, and Joseph was worried about Mary. Her baby was due soon. But they had to go.

When they got to Bethlehem, the town
was full of people.

There wasn't one spare room.

There wasn't one spare bed, not
anywhere.

Even the inn was full.

But Mary's baby was coming *soon*.
They had to find *somewhere* to stay.

There was only one place left: the place where the animals slept!

They got there just in time. *Very* soon, Mary's baby was born.

There was no place for him to sleep, except a manger, where the animals were fed. Joseph filled it with clean straw, while Mary wrapped her baby tight.

Safe in the manger, little Jesus slept…

Outside on the hills, the sheep were safe
in their pen. A strong stone wall with
prickly thorns on top kept the fierce wild
animals out. And all night long the
shepherds watched out for danger.

All was dark.

All was quiet.

Then suddenly the sky blazed with light, too bright to look at. An angel was standing there. He spoke to the shepherds in a loud, clear voice:

"Good news! The best news ever! For you and the whole world!

"Today, in Bethlehem, your King is born. God's promised King! Go, and see for yourselves! You will find him lying in a manger!"

At once the sky was full of angel voices:
    "Glory to God in heaven –
    and peace on earth!"

Then, once again, all was dark; all was
quiet.
    The shepherds took a deep breath.
    "We must do as the angel said. The
sheep will be safe enough." And they
hurried off to Bethlehem.

There they found the new-born King, just as the angel had told them.

Not in a palace.

Not in a house.

Not even in the inn.

They found him lying in a manger, in the place where the animals slept.

The shepherds told Mary and Joseph all
that had happened:
   "Suddenly the sky blazed with light,
and an angel spoke to us!
   " 'Today, in Bethlehem,' he said, 'your
King is born. God's promised King! Go,
and see for yourselves!' "
   Mary listened. This was a night to
remember. She would never forget it.

The shepherds strode back through the dark streets. Soon it would be morning. They must see to their sheep.

The people of Bethlehem heard them go by. Deep, strong shepherd voices singing God's praise: the first Christmas carols!

35

Presents for Christmas

Some visitors came riding to Jerusalem.
   Bang! Bang!
   They knocked at the palace door.
   "We've come to see the king," they said, "the king who has just been born."
   King Herod was *most* upset. A new king? Instead of him? Never!

The men bowed low before him.

"We have come from the east," they said. "We saw a bright new star, and followed it here. A new star for a new king–a king for your people, the Jews. We have come so far to see him. Please tell us where he is."

King Herod was MOST upset. Who could this new king be? Then he remembered something. He sent for his wise men.

"Long ago, God promised to send a king," he said. "Do you know where that king will be born?"

"In Bethlehem, sire," they answered. "So say the prophets of old."

King Herod wanted to find the new king.
He wanted to *kill* him! But he was much
too cunning to say so.

"You must go to Bethlehem," King
Herod said to the visitors. "When you
find the new king, please let me know.
I would like to see him too."

That night they saw the star again, and
followed it to Bethlehem. It shone in the
sky right over the place where Jesus was.

   "At last, we have found the new king,"
they said, as they knelt down before him.
Then out of their bags came the presents
they had brought him.

"My gift is gold," said the first visitor.

"My gift is frankincense,"* said the second.

"My gift is myrrh,"** said the third.

These were costly presents for a king. Strange things to give a baby!

* This was burned as sweet-smelling incense.

** This was used for anointing, medicine, embalming.

King Herod waited and waited.
But the men did not come back.
God had sent them home by another
road.

The king sent his soldiers to Bethlehem.
  "Kill every boy under two years old,"
he ordered them. "I will have no new
kings in *my* land…"

But Mary and Joseph and Jesus were not there. God had sent an angel to warn them.

"Hurry! Hurry!" the angel said. "It's not safe to stay here."

So they got up in the night and went to a place where King Herod could not hurt them. They did not go home to Nazareth until they heard that King Herod was dead.

36

Where is Jesus?

The little town of Nazareth was buzzing with excitement! They were getting ready for a visit to God's temple in Jerusalem.

The fathers were busy with the packing. The mothers were busy with the food. And the children were everywhere!

Jesus was going for the very first time. He was twelve years old.

When they got there, the city was
crowded. Its narrow streets were packed
with people, *all* going to God's temple.
There was a wall all around the temple,
with big gates–like a castle. Inside was a
big open square and more walls. Joseph
and Jesus crossed the square.

In the shade by the walls the teachers sat. They were telling the people about God and how to please him. They were answering questions. Jesus wanted to stop and listen, but Joseph hurried on.

That night the family had a special meal. They told the story that everyone loved –how God had helped his people to escape from Egypt, long, long ago.*

* This was the Passover Festival; see story 11.

Then it was time to go home.

The fathers were busy with the packing. The mothers were busy with the food. And the children were everywhere!

No one noticed that Jesus was missing –until bedtime.

Jesus was lost!

No one had seen him *all day*.

Mary and Joseph hardly slept, they were so worried. As soon as it was light, they went back to Jerusalem, looking and looking for Jesus.

At last, they came to the temple.

And there he was, safe and sound, with the teachers—listening and asking questions.

"*Jesus!*" Mary cried. "We've been looking for you everywhere. We've been *so* worried."

Jesus looked surprised. He wasn't being naughty. He never did bad things.

"Surely you knew I'd be here. The temple is my Father's house," he said. Jesus knew that God was his Father.

Then he got up at once, and went with them.

37

Down by the River

There was a big crowd, down by the Jordan river. What was happening? Something exciting? The children wriggled to the front to see.

But all they saw was a man, talking!

A very strange man!

He wore thick hairy clothes, with a belt round his middle.

"That's John," one of the grown-ups said. "Zechariah and Elizabeth's boy.

"He's come from the desert. He lives there now. It's a lonely, scary place, and there's not much food. He eats locusts,* and honey from wild bees!"

* An insect like a grasshopper.

John was speaking, loud and fierce.

"Make way! Make way, for God's promised King. He is coming soon–so get ready."

"What must we do?"

"You must stop being greedy," John said, "and share. Stop doing bad things. God has told us the best way to live–so do as he says.* Then you'll be ready for the King."

* See story 13.

The grown-ups all looked ashamed.

"We *have* been greedy and done bad things. But we're sorry—really, truly sorry."

"Then follow me," John said. And he walked right into the river!

One by one, the people followed him into the water. They wanted to get rid of all the bad things they had done.

"God knows that you are really sorry," John said. "He has forgiven you and washed* you clean–inside and out. Go home now, and live as God wants. Then you will be ready for God's King."

At last everyone had been into the water.

But who was *this* coming?

* This special washing, to show that sins are forgiven, is called baptism; so John is known as "the Baptist".

It was *Jesus*.* He stepped into the water.
"You've done nothing wrong," John
said to him. "You should be washing *me!*"
But Jesus said: "We must do all that
God wants us to do."

As Jesus came out of the river, John
heard God say:
"This is my Son. I love him, and I am
pleased with him."

* Now about thirty years old.

38

Twelve Special Friends

"Do you know what Jesus is saying?
Come and hear."
   "Do you know what Jesus is doing?
Come and see."

God had given Jesus special work to do.
Everyone came to hear what Jesus was
saying. Everyone came to see what Jesus
was doing. They brought people who
were ill–and Jesus made them well again!

"Good news!" Jesus said. "God has sent me to bring good news:

"Good news for those who are poor.

"Good news for those who have been taken prisoner–they will be set free!

"Good news for those who cannot see–soon their eyes will be opened!

"The time has come for God to rescue his people and make them safe."

Jesus stood on the beach by the lake.
Lake Galilee was so big it was like the sea.

He watched the fishermen cleaning their nets.

"Come with me, and catch bigger fish!" Jesus called to Peter and Andrew.

"Come with me, and catch bigger fish!" he called to James and John.

Jesus didn't mean the fish in the lake.
He meant *people*!

   He wanted Peter and Andrew, James
and John to help him tell everyone God's
good news. They were the first four
special friends of Jesus.

Matthew was sitting at his table, counting his money. He was a tax-man.

"Pay up! Pay up!" he said. "The Emperor wants his tax."

All the nice people thought Matthew was bad. He helped the Emperor and he helped himself!* They would not be friends with him.

But Jesus wanted Matthew to be one of his special friends.

"Come with me," he said. And Matthew left his money and came!

* By collecting more tax than was due.

Matthew gave a party for Jesus at his
house. All the nice people grumbled.

"Jesus is good. How can he be friends
with bad people?"

But Jesus said, "They need me. I've
come to help the people who need me,
not those who think they are good
already."

Jesus had five special friends:
   Peter and Andrew,
   James and John,
   and Matthew.
But that still wasn't enough. He talked to
God about it–then he chose seven more:
   Thomas and Philip and Bartholomew,
   Thaddaeus and *another* James,
   Simon and Judas.
   That made TWELVE special friends.*

* The twelve "apostles": "sent" by Jesus to tell the good news.

Jesus and his twelve special friends went to all the towns and villages, telling everyone God's good news.

Mary, Joanna, Susanna and some others took care of Jesus and his special friends. *All* helping to tell God's good news.

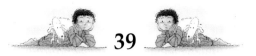

39

The Very Scary Storm

Wheeooeee! howled the wind.
Wheeooeee!

The little boat was right in the middle of the lake when the wind began to howl. Lake Galilee was so big it was like the sea.

"It's a lovely day," Jesus had said to his special friends that morning. "Let's go across the lake." They had been so busy, they needed a day off.

The sun was warm, and the lake was still
—*so* still, that Jesus lay down in the boat
and fell fast asleep.

Then, all of a sudden, the wind began
to howl: Wheeooeee! Wheeooeee!

And the lake wasn't still now. It was
full of big waves that tossed the little
boat up and down. Big waves that came
toppling over the sides.

The boat began to sink…

"Wake up! Wake up!" said Jesus'
special friends. "Save us–we're sinking!"
They were *very* scared. They had never
seen such a storm.

But Jesus was not a bit scared.

"Gently, gently now!" he said to the
howling wind. "Look what you're
doing!"

"Lie down! Lie down!" he said to the
waves. "You're upsetting the boat!"

And at once the wind stopped howling
and the waves stopped tossing.
All was quiet and still again.

The friends all looked at one another.
None of them could have done that!
How had Jesus done it?
"Why were you all so frightened,"
Jesus said, "when you know that God is
looking after you? *Trust* him!"

40

The Two Houses

Jesus was telling a story. Everyone was
listening. They were out on the hillside
close to the lake.

Once upon a time, there were two men.
One man said: "I want to build a house.
I'll build it on the rock: that's a good, safe
place." So he dug and dug, down to the
rock, and he built his house there.

Then the rain fell
and the wind blew
and the floods came…
But his house stood safe on the rock.

"If you listen to me, and do as I say,"
Jesus said, "you are like that man."

The other man said: "I want to build a house. I'll build it on the sand, where it's easy to dig." His house was soon built.
    Then the rain fell
    and the wind blew
    and the floods came...
And his house fell down with a CRASH!

"If you listen to me, but *forget* what I say," Jesus said, "you are like that man."

Jesus' special friends sat close, as he told them the secrets of God's Kingdom:

"God blesses the people who know that
they need him:
they belong to God's Kingdom.
God blesses those who are sad:
he will comfort them.
God blesses those who want to do right:
he will give them what they want.
God blesses those who mend quarrels:
they will be called God's children,
because they are like him."

"Long ago," Jesus said, "God told his people the best way to live. This is what you must do:

"Love your enemies,
not just your friends.
Be kind to everyone, and share.
Be as nice to other people
as you want them to be to you.
For God takes care of *everyone*
–nice and nasty, good and bad."

The hot sun shone on the blue lake. The wild flowers in the grass glowed bright as jewels. Birds hopped close, hoping for crumbs.

But the grown-ups were worried. They didn't have much money.

"What are we going to eat? The children are hungry. And what are we going to wear—our clothes are worn out?" They couldn't stop worrying.

"There's no *need* to worry!" Jesus said to them.

"Just look around you. God gives the birds their food. And see those flowers! Could anyone have more beautiful clothes?

"If God looks after the birds and the flowers, he's sure to look after you. You matter so much more to him!

"Forget your worries. Love God and do as he wants. And God will give you what you really need."

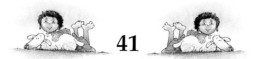

41

A Great Idea

There was a man who could not walk. He could not even get up.

"How I wish I could be like you," he said to his friends.

The man could not walk—but he had four good friends to help him. One day his friends had a great idea.

"We'll take you to Jesus," they said. "Jesus will make you well!"

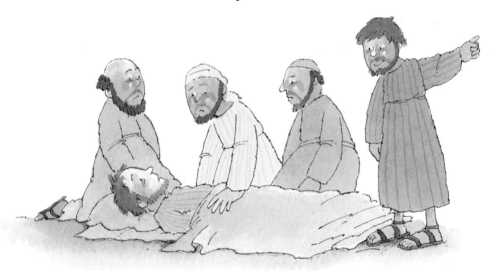

So they picked the man up on his bed-
mat, and carried him to the house where
Jesus was.

But there was such a crowd at the door,
they couldn't get near.

"Let's try the stairs," said one of the
friends. (The stairs were outside the
house.) So they went up… right up…

…to the roof! The house had a flat roof made of dry mud and sticks.

When they got there, the friends began to dig! They dug and dug, *right through* the roof! They made a great big hole. Then they let the man down on his bed-mat, until there he was…

…right next to Jesus!

Jesus looked down at the man. He looked up at the four good friends–and he smiled.

"You want me to make him well," Jesus said. "And so I will–completely well!"

Then he said to the man:

"Every bad thing you have done is forgiven. Now, up you get. Pick up that mat. You can walk home!"

And so he did!

42

The Kind Soldier

The soldier was very upset. One of his
servants was ill–so ill, not even the
doctors could help. The soldier was very
upset, but what could he do?

"Excuse me, sir," said one of his men.
"Have you heard about Jesus? They say
he can cure all kinds of illness."

"Then I must find him at once," the
soldier said. "There's no time to lose."

The soldier hurried off. He found Jesus, with a crowd of people round him.

"My servant has a bad pain," the soldier said to Jesus. "He is so ill, not even the doctors can help him."

"*I* can help him," Jesus said. "I'll come home with you now, and make him better."

"Please don't go to all that trouble.
I don't deserve it," the soldier replied.
"Just say the word. When I give an order,
my men all do as I say.* So I know my
servant will get well if you just say the
word."

He was so *sure* that Jesus could make
his servant better!

* He was a centurion, a Roman army officer in charge of 100 men.

Jesus was very surprised. He had never met anyone quite as sure as this Roman soldier.

"You can go home now," Jesus said to him. "You will find your servant well again–because you were so sure I could make him better."

So the soldier went home–and found his servant well again, just as Jesus said.

43

Jesus and the Little Girl

Jairus loved his little girl dearly. She was just twelve years old.

But one day, when he came home, she wasn't there to meet him. The house was all quiet.

"Our little girl is ill," her mother said. There were tears in her eyes. "She's *terribly* ill. I'm so afraid…"

Jairus was frightened too. His little girl
might die! He must try to save her. So he
set off at once to find Jesus.

"Please come and see my little girl," he
said. "If you don't, I think she will die."

"I'll come," Jesus said. But it was a
long walk from the lake, and there were
crowds of people.

"*Please* hurry!" Jairus begged. He was so worried. But people kept stopping Jesus and he could not hurry.

Then a message came for Jairus: "It's too late. Your little girl has died."

"Don't worry," Jesus said at once. "Just trust me."

Jesus took Peter and James and John – three of his special friends – and they came to Jairus' house.

Everyone there was making a great noise, crying.

"She's not dead – she's only asleep," Jesus said. But they just laughed at him. They knew she was dead.

Jesus went to the little girl's room, with her mother and father, and Peter, James and John. He sent everyone else away.

The little girl was lying on her bed. *So* still.

Then Jesus took her by the hand. "Get up, little girl," he said.

She opened her eyes. Who were all these people?

Then, as if she had just woken up, she got out of bed.

Her mother and father could hardly believe it. Their little girl was *alive* again!

"Give her something to eat," Jesus said, gently. And her mother went out to the kitchen, her face one great big smile, she was so happy.

44

A Farmer Went to Sow...

Jesus was telling everyone God's good
news. People came from far and near to
listen. He told them stories. That was fun.
　　Jesus' stories helped people learn
about God: they made them think and
ask questions. He began his story...

A farmer went to sow. He scattered the seeds from his bag.

Some fell on the path, where the birds just gobbled them up.

Some fell among stones. They began to grow, but the stones got in the way. The little plants drooped and died in the baking sun.

Some fell among thorns that grew up and choked them.

But some seeds fell into good rich earth. Each of those seeds made a big strong plant. And every plant made more new seeds–thirty, or sixty or a hundred times more than the farmer sowed.

"What does the story mean?" asked Jesus' special friends. "Please tell us."

"It's about what happens when people hear the good news about God's Kingdom," Jesus said. "Some people don't really listen at all. So it's snatched away, like the seed the birds gobbled up.

"Some people are glad to hear it–but only at first. When trouble comes, they are like the little plants that drooped and died in the baking sun.

"Some people are so worried about the things they need, or so busy getting rich, that there's no space left for the seed of the good news to grow. That's like the seed that was choked by thorns.

"But some people really listen and learn. They are like the plants that made more new seeds—thirty, or sixty, or a hundred times more than the farmer sowed."

"We want to be like that," thought Jesus' special friends.

"Please tell us more about God's Kingdom," they said to him.

"It's like a tiny seed," Jesus said. "You can hardly see it now. But it will grow and grow, as a little seed grows into a great big tree.

"God's Kingdom is like finding buried treasure, or a beautiful jewel. It's so special, you want to keep it, no matter how much it costs."

"That's *really* good news!" said Jesus' special friends. "We must tell everyone the good news of God's Kingdom."

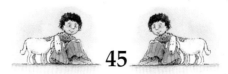

45
The Big Picnic

It was getting late. A big crowd of people had listened to Jesus all day. Now everyone was tired and hungry.

"There's nothing here for them to eat," said Jesus' special friends. (They were out in the hills, in a lonely place.) "They must go to the farms and villages, and buy something there."

"*You* give them something to eat," Jesus said.

"We couldn't buy food for all these people—it would cost far too much," Philip said. There were more than *five thousand* people!

"Ask if they have any bread," said Jesus.

So Jesus' special friends went all round
that great big crowd.

"Have you got any bread?"

"Have *you* got any bread?"

But they all shook their heads—except
for one small boy. He had five bread rolls
and two small fish to eat for his dinner.

Andrew took him to Jesus.

"Here's a boy who has five bread rolls
and two small fish. But they won't go far
among all these people."

The little boy was *very* hungry. He
looked down at his dinner. Then he
looked up at Jesus. Without a word, he
held out his five bread rolls and two
small fish for Jesus to take.

Jesus smiled at him. And the little boy felt so happy. He had done the right thing.

Jesus always said thank you to God for his food. So now he thanked God for the little boy's dinner.

After that, he shared it with *all* the people.

First the bread, and then the fish.

The little boy couldn't believe his eyes.

Every one of those people got a share!

Not just a crumb, but plenty of dinner for them all.

Not just enough, but lots left over. Jesus' special friends filled *twelve baskets* with left-overs!

"Everyone needs bread to eat," Jesus said. "But you need *me* even more."

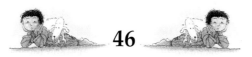

46

"Help! Help!"

People were always asking Jesus questions. One day a teacher came to him.

"I know we must love God," he said. "And I know that God wants us to take care of other people, too. But who does he want us to help? Is it our friends? Or the people we know?"

Then Jesus told him this story…

Once upon a time, a man was walking
down a lonely road. All of a sudden,
some big, bad robbers jumped out at him.

"Help! Help!" cried the man–but there
was no one to hear him.

Those big, bad robbers hit the man and
hurt him. Then they took all his money
and ran away.

He was left at the side of the road.

"Oh! Ooh!" groaned the man. He hurt all over. He couldn't get up. He lay there in the burning sun. He couldn't do anything.

Then he heard footsteps.

Nearer and nearer the footsteps came.

"Help, at last," thought the man. But the footsteps went on by. Someone had seen him, but they hadn't come to help!

"Oh! OOH!" groaned the man. He was feeling dreadful.

A long time passed.

Then he heard footsteps again.

Nearer and nearer the footsteps came.

"Help, at last," thought the man. But the footsteps went on by. Someone else had seen him, but they hadn't come to help. The man was feeling worse and worse.

It was getting late when he heard a new sound.

Clip clop! Clip clop!

Someone was coming down the road on a donkey. This was a man from another country, an enemy country. But he stopped when he saw the man who was hurt.

"He needs help," the traveller said.

So he cleaned the man's cuts and put on
bandages. Then he lifted him carefully
onto his donkey.

A little way on, they came to an inn.

"This poor man has been hurt by some
big bad robbers. They've run off with all
his money," the traveller told the innkeeper. "We must take good care of him."

Next day, he had to go on. He hadn't
finished his journey.

"Here's some money," the traveller
said to the innkeeper. "I hope it's enough.
Take care of the man until he is well. If it
costs more, I will pay you when I come
back."

Now Jesus asked the teacher a question.

"Tell me, which of those people did as God wanted?"

"The one who was kind and helped the man who was hurt," the teacher answered.

"Then be like him," said Jesus. "Be kind to anyone who needs your help. Not just your friends. Not just the people you know. But *anyone*."

47

The Lost Sheep

Wherever Jesus went, there were crowds of people–good people and bad people, too. They wanted to see what he did. They wanted to hear what he said.

Many people loved Jesus. But some of them grumbled.

"Jesus is friends with a lot of bad people. He goes to their parties. That's not right."

So Jesus told this story…

Once upon a time a man was counting his sheep. He had a *hundred* sheep, so it took a long time.

"One, two, three…

"twenty… thirty… forty…

"ninety-seven, ninety-eight, ninety-nine…"

Where was number 100?
Number 100 was lost!

He had ninety-nine sheep left. So did he
mind that one was lost? Of course he did!
   The man went out at once to look for it.
He looked and he listened. He listened
and he looked. He wouldn't give up till
he found his lost sheep.
   At last he heard a tiny sound.
Baaa! Baaaaa!

He followed the sound – and there was his
sheep!

He gave it a big hug.

Then he picked the sheep up. He put it
across his shoulders. And he carried that
sheep all the way home.

When he got to his house, he rushed
indoors to tell his wife and children:
"I've found it! The lost sheep is safe!"
Then he hurried next door.
"I've found it! The lost sheep is safe!
Come to my house for a party."

Everyone smiled. The story had a happy ending. Then Jesus turned to the grumblers:

"If you lose a sheep, aren't you glad to find it? When someone in trouble comes back to God, God is happy too. God doesn't want *anyone* to be lost."

Jesus talked some more about sheep and the shepherd who looks after them:

"A good shepherd knows each one of his sheep. And they know his voice. The sheep will follow their shepherd–but they run away from strangers."

Then Jesus said:

"I am the good shepherd,
I know my sheep and my sheep know me."

"If a fierce wild animal comes to hurt the sheep," Jesus said, "a good shepherd fights it. He never runs away."
Then he said:

"I am the good shepherd,
I will die for my sheep, to keep them safe."

48
Lost–and Found

"Jesus is friends with a lot of bad people. That's not right," the grumblers kept on saying.

"But God loves and cares about *everyone*, not just good people," Jesus said. And he told them this story…

Once upon a time, there was a father who had two sons. The older boy helped on the farm. But the younger one said:

"Give me my share of your money – now. I want to have some fun."

That made his father sad. But he gave him the money. The boy left home and went far away.

The fun didn't last: his money was soon spent. The boy got a job. It was feeding the pigs. He was *so* hungry he could have eaten the pig-food!

He was very unhappy too.

"This is silly," he thought at last. "Why don't I go home? No one's hungry there. I'll tell Dad I'm sorry I wasted all his money. I don't deserve to be one of the family. But perhaps he'll let me work for him." So he set off for home.

All this time his father had waited and watched for his boy to come home. Now here he was, coming down the road!

He ran out to meet him.

"I'm sorry, Dad. I'm *so* sorry," the boy said. "I don't deserve to be one of the family." But his father just hugged him and kissed him.

"Fetch the boy some clothes," he shouted. "Dress him up! We're going to have a party! My boy has come home, and I'm so happy! I thought I had lost him—but now he is found."

"Whatever is going on?" the older boy asked, when he came in from work.

"Your brother has come home, and your father is giving him a party," they told him.

"A party! After all the trouble he's caused! Dad's never given *me* a party. It's not fair!"

He wasn't a bit pleased. He was *very* grumpy.

But his father said to him:

"You know I love you. I will always love you. One day everything I have will be yours. Please don't sulk. Today is a day to be glad. Your brother has come home, and I'm so happy. I thought I had lost him—but now he is found!"

49

"Our Father..."

Every day, Jesus said his prayers. He loved to talk to God.

"Please teach us how to talk to God," said his special friends.

So Jesus taught them this prayer:

"Our Father God…
Come, and be our King for ever:
then everyone will do as you want.
Give us each day
the things we really need.
Forgive us for the bad things that we do,
as we forgive everyone who hurts us.
And keep us from all harm."

"It's good to be good," Jesus said. "But you mustn't show off about it." And he told them a story…

Once upon a time, two men went to God's temple to pray. One of them was pleased with himself. He thought he was keeping all God's rules for the best way to live. The other was a cheat.

"I never tell lies," the first man boasted to God. "I'm not greedy. And I never ever cheat. Not like that man over there." He was *so* proud of himself.

The other man was ashamed of himself, and hung his head. He was *so* sorry for what he had done.

"I'm a really bad person," he said to God. "I know I don't deserve it—but please forgive me."

"God was pleased with *that* man," Jesus said, "and forgave him, because he was sorry."

Some mothers brought their children to
Jesus. They wanted him to ask God to
bless them.

But Jesus' special friends tried to send
them away.

"Stop bothering Jesus," they said to the
mothers. "Can't you see he's busy?" They
didn't think mothers and children were
very important.

But Jesus did.

"You mustn't stop them," Jesus said to his special friends. "Let them come. God wants children as well as grown-ups in his Kingdom.

"You must *all* be like loving, trusting children," Jesus said, "if you want to belong to God's Kingdom."

50

The Best Party Ever

One day, when Jesus was at a party, someone said to him:

"The party I *really* want to go to is the one in God's Kingdom. That will be the best party ever."

Jesus was always inviting people to belong to God's Kingdom. He knew that God wanted everyone to be there and enjoy that special party. So he told this story…

Once upon a time, a man decided to give a big party. He asked lots of people to come. Then he began to get ready.

Sweep and clean! Sweep and clean! All through the house.

They cooked lots of yummy, scrummy food.

Sizzle, sizzle! Stir and taste!

At last everything was done.

"Go and tell the people it's time to come to my party," the man said to his servants.

But what did those people do, when they heard?

One by one, they began to make excuses! They didn't want to stop what they were doing. They didn't really *want* to come!

The man was very angry.

"If *they* won't come," he said, "go into the town and find some people who will."

So they went into the town. There were lots of hungry people there. Poor people. People who couldn't walk. People who couldn't see.

"Come to the party," they said. And all those people came.

But still there was room.

So they went into the country. There were lots of hungry people there, too. People tramping the roads. People with no homes to go to.

"Come to the party," the man's servants said. And all those people came.

Now the house was *full* of people. How they enjoyed that party!

But none of the people the man asked
first were there. They didn't taste a
mouthful of that yummy, scrummy food.

They were asked to come. But they
didn't say yes. So they missed all the fun
of the party.

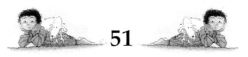

51

"Who Am I?"

"Who do you think I really am?" Jesus asked his special friends one day.

They had been his friends for a long time now. They had seen him make people well. They had listened to all he said about God and his Kingdom.

Peter was quick to answer.

"You are the promised King," he said. "God has sent you to rescue us and make us safe."

Jesus was pleased with Peter's answer. He was glad they knew who he really was.

"You are my friends," Jesus said. "I have lots of friends. But I have enemies too—and they are going to kill me."

"No! No! You mustn't let them!" Peter cried. "Surely God won't let them?"

Jesus was God's promised King. He had to rescue his people and make them safe. How could he be killed?

"I must do whatever God wants," Jesus said. "But never fear. I will come to life again."

Jesus took Peter and James and John up
a big mountain. He wanted a quiet talk
with God.

While they were there, something very
strange happened.

Jesus' face began to shine–brighter and
brighter, like the sun. His clothes were
white as white.

Then a misty cloud rolled over the mountain and they couldn't see him any more. But they heard a voice:

"This is my own Son, whom I love," said the voice. "Listen to what he says."

And they knew it was God!

Peter, James and John were *so* scared, they hid their faces. They didn't dare look.

Then someone gently touched them. It was Jesus. And he looked just the same as always!

"Don't be afraid," he said.

As they came down the mountain, Jesus said:

"Don't tell anyone what you have seen, or what you have heard. Not yet. It's a secret."

"I Can See!"

"Spare some money! Give some money to a poor blind beggar!" Bartimaeus cried.

He had bad eyes and he couldn't see. Everything was dark.

All day long, he sat by the dusty, dirty road. All day, every day. He couldn't see to work. So he had to ask for money.

Then, one day, Jesus came to the town where Bartimaeus lived. Bartimaeus knew that Jesus made people well. Perhaps Jesus would make him see!

There were voices. Loud, excited voices.
Bartimaeus could hear people coming.
    Slap, slap! Patter, patter!
Bartimaeus could hear their feet.
    "Help me, Jesus! Help me, Jesus!" he
shouted at the top of his voice.
    Jesus heard, and he stopped.

"Tell him to come here," Jesus said.

"Jesus wants to see you," they told blind Bartimaeus.

At once, he threw off the coat that kept him warm. He jumped up and ran to Jesus. He couldn't see, but people helped him find his way.

"What do you want me to do?" Jesus asked him.

"I want to see. Please make me see!"

"You trusted me to make you better," Jesus said. "So you *shall* see."

Bartimaeus opened his eyes wide. It wasn't dark any more. It was light!

"I can see! I can *see!*" he shouted in delight. "I'm coming with you, Jesus!"

Jesus said:

"I am the light of the world,
It is never dark where I am.
Come with me and walk in the light."

53

A Nasty Little Cheat

Zacchaeus stretched up–up–to the
lowest branch of the tree. He could only
just reach, he was such a little man.
    He began to climb…

Zacchaeus wanted to see Jesus. But there
were *so* many people. They were bigger
than he was, and he couldn't see past
them. So he said to himself, "I'll climb that
tree. I'll be able to see him from there."

Jesus came by. Zacchaeus looked right
down at him from his tree.

To his surprise Jesus stopped. He
looked right up at Zacchaeus.

"Come down from that tree!" Jesus
said, with a big smile. "I want to come to
your house today!" He said it as if they
were friends already.

Zacchaeus was *very* excited. He was rich, but no one wanted to be friends with him. Zacchaeus was a tax-man and a cheat. When he came to collect people's tax-money, he made them pay too much.

"How can Jesus go to that man's house?" everyone grumbled. "Zacchaeus is nothing but a nasty little cheat."

But Zacchaeus stopped cheating. Jesus was his friend now: he wouldn't like it.

"I shall give half my money to the people who don't have enough," he said to Jesus, later that day. "And I'll pay back everyone I've cheated–*four times* as much as I took."

"It's people like you I want to rescue and bring back to God," Jesus said. He was *very* pleased.

54

Little House at Bethany

Jesus went to Jerusalem. It was Festival*
time and the city was full of people. So he
stayed at the house in Bethany, where
Martha and Mary and Lazarus lived. It
wasn't far away.

Martha was always busy, busy, cooking
and cleaning the house.

"Tell Mary she must help me," Martha
said to Jesus—all hot and flustered.

* The yearly springtime Passover Festival.

But Mary was listening to Jesus. She didn't want to miss a word. Jesus wanted Martha to listen too. He didn't need a special meal. He didn't mind a bit of dust.

Martha and Mary and Lazarus loved Jesus very much, and he loved them.

One dreadful day, Lazarus was ill. Martha and Mary sent a message to Jesus: "Please come quickly, or he'll die."

But Jesus didn't get there in time–and Lazarus *did* die.

Martha came to meet Jesus. Her eyes were all red with crying.

"If *only* you had come quickly," she said. "God will do anything you ask him. You could have made Lazarus well. But now he's dead and buried."

Mary said the same:

"If *only* you had come quickly." They began to cry again.

Jesus cried too. But he had a surprise for Martha and Mary. A very BIG surprise.

"Lazarus will come to life again," Jesus said. "God wants it to happen. And listen, here's the best news of all:

"Everyone who trusts me will live, *even if they die."*

Jesus stood outside the cave where Lazarus was buried.

"Lazarus, come out!" Jesus called. And Lazarus did!

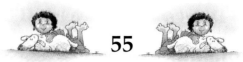

55

A Donkey for the King

"You'll find a young donkey in the village over there," Jesus said to his special friends. They were going to Jerusalem.

"Tell the donkey's master that I need it. And bring the donkey here."

Jesus sat on the donkey's back. No one had ever done that before. But the little donkey didn't kick or jump.

Crowds of people came to meet Jesus.
They knew all about him. They were very
excited. They laughed and cheered and
shouted for joy:
"Hooray! Hooray!
Here comes God's promised King!*
God bless our King!"

They came to the temple. The donkey had
done well. He could go home now.

* He came on a donkey as a sign of peace.

The temple was a special place. A quiet place for people to say their prayers. A place where God could talk to them.

So what was all that NOISE?

Roo-coo! Roo-coo!

"Buy a pair of pigeons!"*

Baaa-maaa! Baaa-maaa!

"Lambs for sale!* Buy a lamb!"

"Get your temple money here!"**

* People bought pigeons and lambs to sacrifice at the temple.
** There was a temple tax, paid in special temple money.

God's temple had been turned into a market! Stalls everywhere. People shouting.

Jesus was *very* angry.

"God's temple is a place to pray," he said, "not to buy and sell—and cheat people! *You robbers!*"

He overturned the stalls. Money rolled everywhere. The pigeons flew up in a fright. The lambs all bleated and ran.

The men in charge of the temple were furious with Jesus.

But blind people came to him. And people who couldn't walk properly. And Jesus made them well.

The men in charge of the temple didn't like that either. They were jealous.

"We must get rid of Jesus," they said.
But they couldn't think how.

Then Judas came to see them.

Jesus had chosen Judas to be one of his
twelve special friends. But Judas wasn't
friends with Jesus any more. So…

whisper, whisper, whisper…

they made a secret plan.

56

A Last Meal Together

It was the day of the Festival, when God's people remembered how he had rescued them from Egypt, long ago.

"Where shall we have our special meal?" asked the twelve friends–and Jesus told them the place.

Before they sat down to supper, Jesus got a bowl of water and a towel. He was their leader, but he knelt and washed their dusty, smelly feet.

Peter didn't think that was right.

But Jesus said:

"If I don't mind doing the nasty jobs, you mustn't either. I want you to take real care of one another, the way I take care of you. Sometimes that means doing things no one likes to do."

It was supper-time. Jesus and his friends sat down to eat.

Jesus took some bread, thanked God for it, and broke it in pieces for them all to share.

"This is my body, given for you," he said.

He took a cup of wine, thanked God for it, and passed it around.

"This is my blood—my life, poured out to make you safe. By my death I shall bring many people back to God."

It was dark. Judas had gone out already
to tell the enemies of Jesus where to find
him.

"Before the night is over," Jesus said,
"every one of you will leave me."

"Not me!" said Peter. "I never will!"

"Yes, even you," Jesus said. "Before the
night is over."

The friends were so sad. They didn't
want Jesus to die. He tried to cheer them
up.

"I am going home, to God my Father," Jesus said. "But I am coming back. One day I will take you to be with God for ever. You all trust God. Now you must trust me. I will always love you.

"If you really love me, you will love one another. I have shown you the way.

"When I've gone," Jesus said, "God will send you his Special Helper.* He will be with you always, wherever you go."

* The Holy Spirit–the Spirit of God himself.

Then they went out for a walk to the
Orchard of Olive Trees.* It was dark and
quiet there, among the old grey trees.

Jesus began to talk to God.

"Father, you can do anything. Please
save me from this terrible death. Unless it
has to be. Do what *you* want."

* The "Garden" of Gethsemane.

Suddenly, torches flared among the trees. People were coming. Soldiers, with clubs and swords!

And Judas leading them.

"*Jesus!*" he said—and he kissed him on the cheek.

It was a signal to the soldiers. They took Jesus prisoner.

His friends tried to help. But Jesus did not want any fighting. So they ran off and left him.

Peter was scared, but he followed the soldiers. They took Jesus straight to the men who wanted to kill him. Peter stood outside in the cold.

"Aren't you one of the prisoner's friends?" someone asked him.

"Not me," Peter answered. *Three times* he said he did not know Jesus – he was *so* scared. But afterwards he was very sorry, and so ashamed that he burst into tears.

57

The Saddest Day

Questions, questions, questions. All night long, Jesus' enemies asked him angry questions. Then, early in the morning, they took him to the Roman Governor.*

"Jesus has done nothing wrong," the Governor said. He wanted to let Jesus go. But the crowd would not let him.

* Pontius Pilate, put in charge by the Roman Emperor.

"Kill him! Nail him to a cross!" the crowd shouted angrily.

It was *Jesus* they wanted to kill!

But why? Jesus was good. He had done nothing wrong.

These people hated Jesus.

"He tells lies about God," they said.

They did not believe he really was God's promised King.

The Governor was afraid of them. At last he said:

"I will do as you want. But don't blame me." And he handed Jesus over to his soldiers.

They took him to Skull Hill and nailed him to a cross. There were two other prisoners on crosses, one on each side of Jesus.

Above Jesus' head was a notice:
    "Jesus of Nazareth: King of the Jews."

Jesus' mother, Mary, stood close to the
cross, with his special friend John.
    "Look after her for me, John," Jesus
said from the cross. And from that day on
John took care of Mary.

Jesus did not hate the soldiers who nailed
him to the cross. He did not hate his cruel
enemies.

"Father, forgive them," he prayed.

At last Jesus cried: "I have finished my
work."

Then he died.

It was the saddest day.

Two friends took his body to the grave.
It was a kind of cave–with a big, heavy
stone across the opening.

Sadly the women watched. It was time
to go home.* But they would come back.

* Because it was Friday, and the sabbath–God's special day
of rest–began at sunset. Christians call the day Jesus died
Good Friday.

58

The Happiest Day

It was early on Sunday morning.* The women were going to Jesus' grave. They had spices to make it all smell nice.

But where was the big, heavy stone? Someone had rolled it away!

The women went inside.

They gasped.

"Jesus' body isn't here! It's gone!"

* This was the first Easter Sunday.

Then they saw a shining angel.

"Don't be afraid," the angel said. "I know you are looking for Jesus. But he isn't here! God has brought him to life again, just as Jesus said. Off you go now, and tell his special friends."

The women ran and ran.
This was the happiest day ever!

They burst into the room.

"He's alive! He's alive!" they shouted. "Jesus is alive! An angel told us. We went to the grave, and his body wasn't there."

The men shook their heads.

"That's just crazy," they said.

But Peter and John went to see for themselves.

John ran faster and got there first. When
Peter caught up, John followed him inside.

Jesus' body had been all wrapped up.
A cloth had been tied round his head. No
one had unwrapped him. The covers
were all there. But the body had gone.
That was how John *knew*.

No one had taken the body away.

JESUS WAS ALIVE!

Peter and John ran to tell the others.

Mary Magdalene was the first to *see* Jesus.
She was standing close to the grave, when
a voice said:

"Why are you crying?"

Her eyes were red and swollen. She
couldn't make out who it was.

Then the voice said: "Mary!" And she
knew. It was *Jesus*.

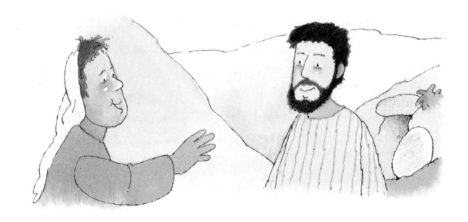

"Go and tell the others," Jesus said.
And off she went, laughing and crying
both at once. She was *so* happy.

That night, Jesus came to see his special friends. They were in the room, talking–and suddenly Jesus was there! They were *very* scared. They thought he was a ghost.

"Don't be afraid," Jesus said. "Look! It's me! Touch me–I'm real." He even ate some supper.

No one was frightened after that. It was the happiest day ever!

All of them were there—except Judas and Thomas.

"I can't believe it was Jesus," said doubting Thomas, when they told him. "I must see for myself where the nails went in. I must touch the place."

The very next week, Jesus came again.

"See, where the nails went in," he said to Thomas. "You can touch the place."

But Thomas didn't need to.

"My Lord," he said, "and my God."

After that, they went back home.

One night, they went fishing on Lake Galilee. But they didn't catch anything.

It was just getting light, when someone called from the beach:

"Have you caught any fish?"

"No, not one," they said.

"Let down the net–on the other side," said the man.

And they caught so many fish, the net almost broke.

"It's Jesus!" John whispered to Peter.

Jesus had lit a fire, all ready for a picnic breakfast. He had fish and bread. And they brought more fish from the boat.

After breakfast, Jesus talked to Peter.
"I want you to take care of my
friends," Jesus said. Peter was *so* pleased.
He had let Jesus down on that dreadful
night. But Jesus still loved him as his
special friend.

59

Jesus Goes Home

"I have done all God wanted me to do,"
Jesus said to his friends.

"Go and tell everyone about me.
Make me lots more friends. Tell them
everything that I have told you: how God
wants to rescue them and make them
safe.

"Wait here until God sends his Special
Helper. Then go, and tell the whole world
about me."

It was nearly time for Jesus to go home to God, his Father.*

"Will you soon be King?" asked his friends. "When will you come back?"

"God will decide," Jesus said.

They were all together** on the Mountain of Olives, near to Jerusalem.

* Forty days had passed since the resurrection; Jesus had been seen many times and in different places by his followers.
** All except Judas, who could not forgive himself for betraying Jesus, and had killed himself.

A cloud came over the mountain, as they talked. They couldn't see Jesus now. Where had he gone?

But two men were there—two angels in shining clothes.

"Why are you looking up at that cloud?" they said. "Jesus has gone home to God, his Father. He will come back—one day—but not now."

Jesus' friends were puzzled.
  "But he told us,

'I will be with you always,
even until the end of the world'

  "…and now he's gone away. So what
did he mean? We shall just have to wait
and see!"

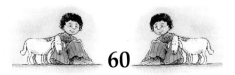

60

When the Wind Blew!

Wheeooeee!

A big wind was coming. In through the door rushed the sound of the wind, and right round the room.

Wheeooeee!

Fire came with the wind. Little flames blew round and came to rest. One flame on every person in the room. But no one was burned.

Jesus' special friends were all together in that room, when the wind came, and the little flames of fire.

Everyone started to talk, all at once. But no one knew the words. They were all speaking strange languages!

God's Special Helper had come!* Now they would be able to tell the whole world about Jesus.

* It was the Day of Pentecost, a harvest festival, fifty days after Passover.

There were lots of visitors in Jerusalem.
They had come from far and wide.

"What's happening? What's
happening?" they asked.

"Someone is telling the wonderful
things that God has done," said one of
them. "I can hear it in my very own
language!"

"So can I! So can I!" said another.

Peter stood up and spoke to the people.

"We have to tell you about Jesus. How God sent him to rescue us and make us safe–and you let him die on a cross."

"What are we to do?" they asked.

"Tell God that you are sorry, and he will forgive you," Peter said. "Then, if you want, you can all be Jesus' friends."

That day, *three thousand* people said, "Yes. We want to be Jesus' friends."

61

Peter's Story

Jesus had told Peter to take care of his friends. And he did.

Peter took care of Jesus' special friends and his new friends, too.

They were making more friends for Jesus every day in the city of Jerusalem!

It was very exciting. They were like one big happy family.

They had meals together. They said
prayers together. And they learned all
about Jesus.

The ones who were rich helped the
ones who were poor. They shared
everything they had.

And God's Special Helper was with
them all. It was like having Jesus always
there, just as he'd promised.

Jesus' enemies wanted to stop Peter
talking about him. But Peter wouldn't
stop. He just went on telling people about
Jesus.

So they put him in prison.

But in the night, God sent an angel
to set Peter free. His friends were so
surprised to see him! They asked God to
help them all be brave and go on telling
people about Jesus.

And God did make them brave. He wanted them to tell *everyone in the world*.

At first Peter thought God meant his own people—the Jews. God had to send him a special dream, to show that he really meant *everyone*.

That same day, three men came to the door: Knock! Knock!

"Captain Cornelius says, please will you come to his house," the men said.

Captain Cornelius was a soldier from Rome. But he loved God. And God had told him to invite Peter home.

God wanted Peter to tell Captain Cornelius and all his friends about Jesus.

So Peter told them everything, from the beginning right up to the dreadful day when Jesus died on a cross.

"But God brought Jesus back to life," Peter said joyfully. "So now, *you* can be his friends too, just like us, if you want."

And right away, God sent his Special Helper to be with these new friends. Just to show that he really does love *everyone* in the world.

62

Paul Meets Jesus

There was a light! A light so dazzling bright it made the sun look pale.

Paul put up his hands to hide his face. The light hurt his eyes. He could not see!

Then he heard a voice:

"Paul! Paul! Why are you being so cruel to me?"

"Tell me who you are," Paul said.

"I am Jesus," answered the voice.

Paul was on his way to the city of Damascus. He was an enemy of the friends of Jesus. He did not believe that Jesus was God's promised King. He did not believe that Jesus was alive again.

"But he *must* be," Paul said, when he heard Jesus' voice. "I was wrong!" He thought of all the cruel things he had done to the friends of Jesus. He was *very, very* sorry.

"Go into the city," Jesus said to Paul. "And I will tell you what to do."

Paul still could not see. Someone had to lead him by the hand.

Jesus sent Ananias to see Paul.

"He's not an enemy any more," Jesus said. "Paul is going to tell *everyone* about me. That's a hard job. But I have chosen him for this special work."

Ananias put his hands on Paul's eyes—
and Paul could see again. He was *so* glad!

So Paul became a friend of Jesus. God
sent his Special Helper to be with him.
And Paul told everyone he met that Jesus
was alive.

"Paul was the cruel enemy of the
friends of Jesus," people said. "But now
he's telling us *all* to be Jesus' friends!"

63

Shipwreck!

Paul had to tell *everyone* the good news about Jesus. That meant a lot of journeys.

Journeys across the sea.

Journeys over the land.

But he didn't go all by himself. He had friends to help him. Everywhere they went, they told the people:

"God wants you to be his friends – that's the good news Jesus came to bring."

Everywhere they went, they made new
friends for Jesus. Paul told them how
much God loved them. He said they must
be kind and loving too:

"Love is the best thing of all.
It makes us kind and patient.
It stops us being boastful and rude and jealous.
It stops us being selfish and cross.
Love makes us loyal: it makes us trust.
Love is for ever and ever."

Some people hated Paul and threw stones
at him. Often he was cold and hungry
and thirsty, and had nowhere to sleep.

But he never gave up. He was always
so glad he could work for Jesus. And Paul
knew that God was helping him. He said:

"Nothing can cut us off from God's love.
Not trouble or hard times.
Not hunger or danger or death.
Nothing in the whole wide world."

After many journeys, Paul went back to Jerusalem. And they put him in prison! How could he tell everyone about Jesus if he was in prison?

"Send me to the Emperor in Rome," Paul said at last. He was sure the Emperor would set him free.*

The city of Rome was far away, across the sea by ship. On the way, a great BIG storm came blowing across the water.

* Paul was a Jew *and* a Roman citizen with the right to be heard by the Emperor.

Wheeooeee! screamed the wind.

Everyone thought they were going to drown. But Paul was not afraid.

"Cheer up!" he said. "God says you will all be safe. So eat some food. You need to be strong."

The ship began to break up.

"Hold on to a bit of the wood," Paul cried. "It will help you to float."

So everyone got safely to land.

When Paul got to Rome, the Emperor was busy. He let Paul live in a house of his own, with a soldier to guard him.

And Paul went right on telling *everyone* the good news about Jesus.

He had lots of visitors. And he wrote letters to the friends of Jesus in all the places he'd been to. He told them more about Jesus. And he answered all their questions. He loved them *so* much.

64

A New World

"One day, I will come back. We will all be together again," Jesus told his special friends before he went home to God.

That was a promise for *all* his friends. One day, some day…

Now, John was on Prison Island.* The friends of Jesus were in trouble.

"Trouble, trouble – will it never end? Why doesn't Jesus come back?" they said.

* The Greek island of Patmos, where prisoners quarried stone.

But God knew all about their trouble.
He sent one of his angels to John.

"Come with me," the angel said.
"I have something to show you."

What he saw was so exciting, John
wrote at once to all the friends of Jesus.

"It's going to be all right," John said.
"God is making everything new again.
He's shown me his wonderful new
world. One day, some day, we will all
share it.

"God will wipe away our tears. No one will die any more. No one will be hurt.

"I saw a beautiful, shining city – the city where God is. It's never dark in that city. It shines all the time with God's light.

"Nothing that's nasty or bad can ever come there. But God's friends can go in and out and enjoy it for ever: God and his people together, as Jesus promised…

"Just as it was when the world began."

WHERE TO FIND…

The quotations in this book

The quoted verses are paraphrases of the Bible text, based on the following passages:

Page 19:   Psalm 136; Psalm 24:1, 2

Pages 122, 123:   The Ten Commandments: Exodus 20

Page 175:   Hannah's Song: 1 Samuel 2

Page 190:   The Lord is my Shepherd: Psalm 23

Page 201:   Psalm 100

Page 213:   David's Lament for Jonathan: 2 Samuel 1

Page 220:   Psalm 150

Page 225:   Proverbs 21:3, 15:4, 12:10, 15:30

Pages 281, 282:   Isaiah 9, 11

Page 291:   Mary's Song (the Magnificat): Luke 1:46–55

Page 337:   The Beatitudes: Matthew 5, Luke 6

Page 338:   The Sermon on the Mount: Matthew 5–7; Luke 6, 12

Page 385:   The Good Shepherd: John 10

Page 393:   The Lord's Prayer: Matthew 6; Luke 11

Page 413:   The Light of the World: John 8

Page 455:   Matthew 28:20

Page 471:   1 Corinthians 13:4–8

Page 472:   Romans 8:35–39

First mention of key people in this book

Aaron 94

Abraham 38

Adam 17

Ahab 232

Ananias 468

Andrew 324

Bartimaeus 410

Benjamin (Ben) 75

Bethuel 53

Boaz 169

Caleb 130

Cornelius 463

Daniel 272

David (171) 188

Delilah 162

Eli 173

Elijah 234

Elisha 251

Elizabeth 288

Esau 56

Eve 17

Gideon 151

Goliath 192

Hannah 172

Herod 302

Isaac 47

Jacob (Israel) 56

Jairus 350

James 324

Jesus 295

Jezebel 232

John 324

John (Baptist) 317

Jonah 264

Jonathan 200

Joseph (NT) 284

Joseph (OT) 74

Joshua 130

Judas 328

Laban 70

Lazarus 418

Leah 71

Martha 418

Mary 284

Mary (2) 418

Mary Magdalene 446

Matthew 326

Miriam 94

Moses 99

Naaman 248

Naomi 164

Noah 28

Paul 466

Peter 324

Philip 328

Rachel 71

Rahab 138

Rebecca 48

Reuben 79

Ruth 165

Samson 156

Samuel (Sam) 173

Sarah 40

Saul 183

Solomon 221

Thomas 328

Zacchaeus 414

Zechariah 290